Kids' Travel Guide to the 10 Commandments

By Carol Mader

Group

Loveland, Colorado

Dedication

This book is dedicated with love to the families who lost children in our violent world during 1999. May this book help right a few wrong paths. With much thanks to the following people for their encouragement, support, and inspiration: Linda Anderson, Shirley Michaels, John Rankin, Bill Hybels, Ray Comfort, Dave Patrick and our prayer group, Leland Lee and our writers' group and to my family. All praise goes to my "Lord [who] stood at my side so that through me the message might be fully proclaimed" (2 Timothy 4:17).

Kids' Travel Guide to the Ten Commandments
Copyright © 2001 Carol Mader

Visit our Web site: **www.group.com**

Credits
Editor: Linda A. Anderson
Creative Development Editor: Karl Leuthauser
Chief Creative Officer: Joani Schultz
Copy Editor: Lyndsay E. Bierce
Art Director: Kari K. Monson
Computer Graphic Artist: Stephen Beer
Illustrator: Brent Cottrell
Cover Art Director: Jeff A. Storm
Cover Designer: wirestone
Production Manager: Peggy Naylor

ISBN 0-7644-2224-3

10 9   10 09 08 07
Printed in the United States of America.

Kids' Travel Guide

Table of Contents

Introduction

In our oscillating world of moral relativism, God's commandments stand as firm as the rocks they were etched into. Children want and need absolute standards. In *Generation Next*, George Barna tells us that 92 percent of Christian teens feel that what is right for one person in a certain situation may not be right for another person in a similar situation. It is only God's unchanging standards for morality that form the foundation of a sane society. Yet this is only one function of the Law.

Simply put, "The law was put in charge to lead us to Christ" (Galatians 3:24a). Let the departure and destination point of your travels be this humbling discovery: We know that through the Law our sin is real, that through the Cross our sin is gone!

This guidebook will lead you and your children into these joyful discoveries. Thank you for your love and dedication in bringing God's Word to wandering young travelers. Teaching God's law is not optional. (See Deuteronomy 11:19.) As our kids journey through their murky gray world, I hope this book will serve as a sentinel crying out, "Oh, that their hearts would be inclined to fear me and keep all my commands always, so that it might go well with them and their children forever!" (Deuteronomy 5:29).

Carol Mader

A Guide to the Guide

This book was designed to be as applicable to kids in grades K–5 as is humanly and divinely possible. So I've interpreted the commandments and built the lessons around points that have to do with a child's world. Even though some groups number the Ten Commandments differently, we have chosen the most widely used numbering approach. During this thirteen-week course, each child may complete a notebook. It will serve as a keepsake so that God's laws become written upon the heart.

Please read each lesson thoroughly, and make a model for the crafts before class. If you do, your lessons will flow much more smoothly. The time recommendations are only guidelines. They will change according to how many are in your group, how prepared you are, and how much help you have.

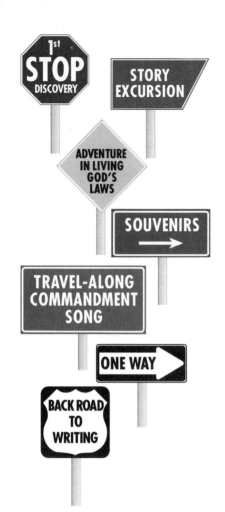

Each lesson starts with a **Departure Prayer.** I've attempted to give you some pointers on prayer, as well as remind you that our work, without God's guidance, is fruitless. **Tour-Guide Tips** are helps for the teacher, and **Scenic Routes** provide more creative options.

First-Stop Discoveries introduce the children to the concepts behind God's commandments. The **Story Excursions** are told in imaginative ways to give your class variety. Choose what you think will best meet your children's needs. The activities in **Adventures in Living God's Laws** lead the children into further application of the point. Each week, ask the children if they had opportunities to obey God's previous commandment. This will be an important faith-growing time.

Souvenirs are paper activities that can go into the children's notebooks. For each lesson, enlarge and photocopy the appropriate commandment from the **"Commandments Page"** handout on page 10. Early-arriving and late-departing kids can color this page.

Please do the **Travel-Along Commandment Song** each week, adding a new verse each week. This will act as a weekly review. The **One-Way Signs** are designed to show the kids how their failure to obey God's law is sin, but our sin leads us to our Savior.

Back Roads to Writing explore the history of the printed word, giving your class an opportunity to write God's commandments in unique ways. You may want to use this time for older kids after the allotted class time. While the kids work on their projects, you can read the **Fun Facts, Did You Know?,** and **Extra Cool** sections to them. Several of the craft ideas in **Back Roads** would require some additional help in the classroom.

Exploring God's Ten Commandments has been a wonderful privilege for me. Teaching them brings a blessing to you. "Whoever practices and teaches these commands will be called great in the kingdom of heaven" (Matthew 5:19b). May you great teachers bring children into a closer and more obedient walk with God. Thank you for being there for them!

Travel-Along Commandment Song

Chant the words of this song to a rap beat.

God gave us loving laws a long time ago. *(Hold hands out as though you're giving a gift.)*

He put them in the Bible so we all would know. *(Clap hands together, then open them as though you're reading a book.)*

If you take a finger and point it high *(point a finger, and raise it high),*

God's first commandment tells you why. *(Point forward.)*

Say this refrain in between each stanza:

Gotta hear me, gotta, gotta hear me.

Gotta hear me, gotta, gotta hear me.

"I am the Lord, your God," says he. *(Point finger up.)*

"You shall have no other gods but *me*!" *(Point to self.)*

Worship God and God alone. *(Hold finger up.)*

You're his flock, his very own. *(Point to heart.)*

"You shall not make an idol" is commandment number two *(hold up right index finger, then left)*,

'Cause second place for God won't do. *(Cross fingers in an X.)*

God wants first place in your life and heart. *(Shade eyes.)*

That's the way to live—that's really smart. *(Hold finger up, like a warning.)*

Our words tell the world what's in our heart. *(Hold up one finger.)*

If you wanna be cool, if you wanna be smart *(hold up two fingers)*,

Speak God's name with love and respect. *(Hold up three fingers.)*

Three fingers keep your words correct. *(Cover mouth with three fingers, then take them away.)*

Hold up four fingers, and push them away *(hold up four fingers, and push away)*

To set aside a special day. *(Slowly move your hand across your chest.)*

Refuel your engines and remember God. *(Wave four fingers on one hand, then the other.)*

Get to a church where he's worshipped and awed. *(Raise hands up.)*

Hey, put your five fingers way down low. *(Push hand down near knees.)*

Honor your parents is the way to go. *(Slowly raise hand.)*

God gave you parents when you were small. *(Slowly raise hand.)*

Respect and obey them while you're growing tall. *(Slowly raise hand.)*

Five fingers for a body, one finger for a sword *(hold up five fingers on right hand and one on left)*—

You shall not kill is the sixth law of the Lord. *("Sword" made from one finger pierces the other hand.)*

Say *no* to violence in TV and shows. *(Hold hands up and push away, like a refusal.)*

Say *yes* to life. It's the way to go! *(Hold hands up and push away.)*

Be true to your husband; be true to your wife. *(Hold up one finger on each hand.)*

Keep your promises all your life. *(Hook fingers together.)*

God told people, "I want to be obeyed. *(Hold up index finger.)*

Remember those promises that you made!" *(Point index finger forward.)*

Ten take away two is eight. *(Hold up both hands, fingers spread apart. Then one hand "steals" two fingers from the other hand.)*

Stealing is a sin God hates. *(Shake head as you hold both hands at sides.)*

Try to be givers, not gimme-gimme getters. *(Hold hands out, then pull them in.)*

Don't be an eighth-commandment forgetter. *(Shake a warning finger.)*

I see ten fingers; you shall not lie. *(Hold up ten fingers.)*

You're number nine; you gotta try *(fold the thumb on one hand into the palm)*

To tell the truth; it's always best. *(Make fists and raise them overhead.)*

God commanded, he didn't suggest. *(Point finger.)*

Put up ten fingers. Pull 'em in, in, in. *(Hold up ten fingers, then close both hands into fists.)*

To want, want, want can be a sin. *(Hold up ten fingers, then make fists.)*

You shall not want what others have got. *(Reach out with hands and then pull in as if grabbing something.)*

Be happy 'cause you've got a lot. *(Make a circle with both hands in front of body.)*

To show God your love, come on, try to obey. *(Hold hands out.)*

But when you mess up, God shows the way. *(Cover face with hands, then move hands away.)*

The commandments point us to the Cross. *(Point up.)*

Jesus died for you. Now make him your boss. *(Make a cross.)*

Stone Tablets

I am the Lord your God.

1. You shall have no other gods before me.

2. You shall not make any idols.

3. Speak God's name with respect.

4. Set aside a special day for God.

5. Honor your father and mother.

6. You shall not kill.

7. Be true to your husband or wife.

8. You shall not steal.

9. You shall not lie.

10. You shall not want what others have.

Commandments Page

For each lesson, enlarge and photocopy the appropriate commandment handout.
Early-arriving and late-departing kids can color the page to add to their notebooks.

1. You shall have no other gods before me.	6. You shall not kill.
2. You shall not make any idols.	7. Be true to your husband or wife.
3. Speak God's name with respect.	8. You shall not steal.
4. Set aside a special day for God.	9. You shall not lie.
5. Honor your father and mother.	10. You shall not want what others have.

Moses Receives the Ten Commandments (Exodus 19–20)

Pathway Point: 🌐 God gave us loving laws to keep us safe.

In-Focus Verse: "Obey carefully all the words of this law. They are not just idle words for you—they are your life" (Deuteronomy 32:46b-47a).

Travel Itinerary

Children want and need boundaries. A life without rules is chaotic and frightening. Like adults, children need to know the perimeters they are free to function within. In *Dr. Dobson Answers Your Questions*, Dr. James Dobson tells a story about a "progressive" educator who wanted to give the children more freedom. He had the chain-link fence taken down around their playground. Rather than feeling independent, the children huddled together near the center of the playground. Their freedom was inhibited by an absence of boundaries.

Rules give us security. In this lesson, the children will discover that it is God's love that motivates him to lay down laws for his people. They'll learn that God is the ultimate parent, putting loving limits on their behavior. As we see from God's words in Deuteronomy 30 and 32, God's laws are not idle words—they are our life!

DEPARTURE PRAYER (up to 5 minutes)

Like any new practice, prayer requires a safety zone. Tell the children that you will pray first, then ask if anyone else wants to pray.

Say: **Dear Lord, you are our Father and maker. You created us, so you know how we need to act. Thank you for giving us loving laws to keep us safe. Thank you for caring enough about us that you didn't leave us in a free-for-all world. Giving us rules proves you love us. Help us to learn what your rules are, why you gave them to us, and how we can make them work in our lives. We love you. Amen.**

1st STOP DISCOVERY (10 minutes) Stop-Sign Safety

Let the children experience life without rules with this active game.

Preparation: Use the materials listed above to make a stop sign. Cut the poster board into an octagon, and cut out white letters that read STOP. Glue the letters to the octagon, and glue or tape the craft stick to the back of the sign. Remove chairs and tables from the room.

Line up half the children (Team A) against one wall and the other half (Team B) against a wall parallel to it. Stand in the middle and say: **When I say "go," I want each team to walk slowly to the opposite wall.** Say "go," and let each group walk to the opposite wall and then back again.

TOUR GUIDE TIP The activities in this book have been designed for multi-age groups. Select from the activities, or adapt them as needed for your class.

TOUR GUIDE TIP Starting a lesson without prayer is like building a tower on sand. Without a solid foundation, it will topple and will have to be rebuilt properly. If you don't have enough time to pray, you don't have enough time to teach! Fight the temptation to dive into the lesson without asking God for his wisdom. Spending a few minutes in prayer can make the difference between wasting your time and watching it produce much fruit. God will give you wisdom to teach as you ask him for it (James 1:5).

Items to Pack: red poster board, scissors, tape, wide craft stick, white paper, glue

Ask:

• **How many of you got bumped?**

Bring out the stop sign. Say: **This time I'm setting up a rule for you. When I say "go," the team that doesn't face a stop sign (Team B) can walk across the room.** Hold the stop sign up for Team A to obey while Team B crosses to the other side. Then hold up the sign for Team B to obey while Team A crosses the room. Have the kids sit down.

Ask:

• **How many of you got bumped this time?**

• **What made the difference?**

• **How is this stop sign like God's commandments or rules?**

• **Why do we have rules?**

Say: **God gave us many rules in his Word, the Bible. We're going to learn about ten special rules called the Ten Commandments.** 🌀 **God gave us loving laws to keep us safe. Let's listen to the Bible story to find out how God gave us his top-ten rules.**

TOUR GUIDE TIP

If your class is small or meets in a very large room, you might want to modify this activity by creating a masking tape square on the floor to define the boundaries. Allow twelve inches of space for each child on each team.

Items to Pack: box of baby wipes, thunder-maker (2 lids to bang together), trumpet or substitute for a trumpet

---

STORY EXCURSION (15 minutes)
Moses Receives the Ten Commandments
(Exodus 19–20)

The class will re-enact the first time God gave his commandments.

Preparation: Think about what you can use to represent Mount Sinai. For example, you can draw a mountain on a chalkboard or throw a blanket over a ladder. To pose as Moses, use a simple costume or a headpiece.

Open your Bible to Exodus 19 and say: **We're going to read our Bible story together. Thousands of years ago, God chose the Israelites to be his special people. They had been slaves in Egypt and cried out to God for help. His loving ears heard their sad cries. With a mighty hand, God led his children—about two million people—out of Egypt. They were free! Moses led the Israelites as they began their journey to a new home.**

Pretend to be Moses, leading the children around the room and ending your "journey" at "Mount Sinai." Say: **Before the Israelites got to their land flowing with milk and honey, God had to teach them what it meant to be his special people. They had to learn how God wanted them to live so they could be safe and happy. He led them out into the desert. They camped next to towering Mount Sinai.**

If the group is small, you can have the kids sit or lie down on carpeting.

The Lord called to Moses from the mountain. If you listen closely, God is about to tell us the dream in his heart. He said, *(use a deep voice)* **"You yourselves have seen how I protected you from the Egyptians and how I carried you as though on eagles' wings and brought you to myself."**

The people responded: "We will do everything the Lord has said." *(Have the kids repeat after you.)*

🌀 **God was about to give his people loving laws to keep them safe. To get the people ready, Moses had them wash their clothes.** *(Give children each a baby wipe, and let them wipe off their clothes.)* **God told Moses that anyone who touched the holy mountain** would die, so Moses built a fence around the mountain. The fence would keep the people safe, just as God's loving laws would keep them safe. *(Let the children line up some chairs in front of your Mount Sinai.)* God wanted the people to know that he was serious. These were not just to be ten good ideas; they were and are today ten holy commandments from the God who made us. Because he made us, he knows what we need to do to be safe and happy.

On the morning of the third day, there was thunder *(bang lids)* and lightning *(flash room lights)*. A thick cloud covered the mountain, and there came a very loud trumpet blast. *(Blow trumpet.)* Everyone in the camp trembled. *(Have all the kids tremble.)* Mount Sinai was covered with smoke. The whole mountain shook violently, and the sound of the trumpet grew louder and louder. *(Blow trumpet.)*

The Lord called to Moses. Moses went up to the top of the mountain, and 🌀 God gave him ten loving laws to keep the Israelites safe. God spoke these words: *(Read Exodus 20:1-17, or read this simpler version.)*

I am the Lord your God.

1. You shall have no other gods before me.

2. You shall not make any idols.

3. Speak God's name with respect.

4. Set aside a special day for God.

5. Honor your father and mother.

6. You shall not kill.

7. Be true to your husband or wife.

8. You shall not steal.

9. You shall not lie.

10. You shall not want what others have.

The people then understood that 🌀 God gave them loving laws for their own good and safety. He gives us the same laws and the same love today.

Ask:

• Why did God give the Israelites the Ten Commandments?

• Why does he give the same commandments to us?

• What do God's laws do for you?

Say: 🌀 God gave the Israelites the Ten Commandments to keep them safe and to create a special people for himself—a family who would love, honor, obey, and respect him.

SCENIC ROUTE →

You can make this story as dramatic as you like. Have someone standing behind a partition speak God's words in a deep voice. Another option is to let the older kids take turns reading the Ten Commandments.

Dry ice "smoke" rolling off the top of Mount Sinai makes this story unforgettable. You can get dry ice at some grocery stores.

(Be sure to use thick gloves when handling dry ice. Make sure children do not touch it.)

If you make Mount Sinai out of a blanket and ladder, you can hide a smaller stepladder behind it so "Moses" can climb to the top.

ADVENTURE IN LIVING GOD'S LAWS

(15 minutes)
A Flock and Fences

Children will build fences to show how God's laws protect them.

Open your Bible to Exodus 19 and say: **Just before he gave the commandments, God said, "Now if you will obey me and keep your part of my contract with you, you shall be my own little flock" (Exodus 19:5, *The Living Bible*). Let's make fences for our flock.**

Items to Pack: modeling dough or plastic clay, bag of cotton balls, and, for each child, 10 wide craft sticks (tongue depressors), 10 miniature craft sticks (2½ inches long)

13

Show the children how to make fences. To make one fence section, glue two wide craft sticks to two miniature craft sticks. Have each child make five fence sections. Have the older children write one commandment on each of the horizontal sections. Let the kids stick the fence posts into pieces of modeling dough so they stand upright. Have each child move his or her fence sections together to form a circle. Scatter the cotton balls on the table outside the fence.

Say: **God chose the Israelites and us to be his special treasure, his very own flock. This is God's dream—to have a special family set apart for himself, safe and happy. Let's pretend that these cotton balls lying outside the fence represent the Israelites. God told them that if they obeyed him, they would be God's special flock. He made a way for *us* to be part of his special flock by sending Jesus.**

Let the each child put a few cotton balls inside the fence to represent the Israelites. Ask:

• **What keeps the flock protected?**

• **How are God's commandments like these fences?**

Say:  **God gave the Israelites loving laws to keep them safe. Unfortunately, they didn't always keep all of God's commandments, just as we don't always follow God's loving laws. God knows that we can't keep all of his commands. That's why Jesus came to pay the price for our sins and become our good shepherd. We become one of God's sheep by believing in Jesus. Following God's loving laws does not make us part of God's flock, but following those laws does keep us safe and happy. It also shows God how much we love him when we try to obey his commands.**

(15 minutes)
On Eagle's Wings

The children will compare a mother eagle to God and watch a "baby eagle fly."

Have each child write on a sheet of paper, "Like a mother eagle, God's loving laws keep me safe." Older kids can help the younger ones write, or the younger children can each draw a picture of an eagle. This paper will represent a mother eagle. Then have each child cut out a 2x5-inch piece from another sheet of paper and fold it in the middle. (Have a sample available for the children to look at.) This will represent the baby eagle.

Gather the children and say: **Before God gave us his loving laws, he said, "You yourselves have seen what I did to Egypt, and how I carried you on eagles' wings and brought you to myself" (Exodus 19:4). This verse refers to an eagle's wings. When a mother eagle teaches her baby to fly, she doesn't just push him out of the nest—she flies beneath her baby to catch him if he falls. Isn't that beautiful? God is like a loving parent, teaching us how to live by giving us loving laws. Let's teach our eaglet to fly while his mother flies below to catch him when he falls.**

Let the children take turns. Two kids will hold either end of the dental floss. One child will place an eaglet (the small folded paper) on the floss and gently guide the eaglet from one end of the floss to the other. Another child will hold the mother (the large piece of paper) and "fly" beneath the baby to catch it if it falls.

After each child has had a turn, ask:

• How would you describe this mother eagle?

• How do God's loving laws remind you of a mother eagle?

• How are you like the baby eaglet?

Say: God is like a loving mother eagle, teaching us how to fly by giving us rules to live by. He doesn't just give us rules; he's there to catch us when we fall (break one of his rules). So  God makes us, gives us loving laws to keep us safe, stays near us, and forgives us when we fail. Isn't God amazing?

 **(15 minutes)**
Safety Gear? Never Fear!
The children will color, cut, and paste the commandments to an illustration of a child to demonstrate that the commandments are meant for our protection.

Hold up the helmet and say: **Sometimes it's a drag to wear a helmet. You have to adjust the straps just right. Sometimes they push into your throat. Sometimes the helmet is hot.**

Ask:

• Why do we bother wearing helmets?

• What would happen if we didn't wear them?

• Why did God bother to give us laws?

• What things do God's laws protect us from?

Give everyone a copy of the "Safety Gear? Never Fear!" handout (page 17), scissors, glue, and crayons. Have the kids cut out the safety gear and glue the helmet, chin strap, and the elbow, knee, and wrist pads to the illustration of the child on the skateboard. The children may also color the pages and add them to their notebooks.

TRAVEL-ALONG COMMANDMENT SONG

Teach your children the first verse of the "Travel-Along Commandment Song." Sing the verse and refrain once yourself, showing kids the accompanying motions, then have the kids join you. Children will be learning a new verse in each ensuing lesson. (The entire song is on pages 6-8.)

God gave us loving laws a long time ago. *(Hold hands out as though you're giving a gift.)*

He put them in the Bible so we all would know. *(Clap hands together, then open them as though you're reading a book.)*

If you take a finger and point it high *(point a finger, and raise it high),*

God's first commandment tells you why. *(Point forward.)*

Gotta hear me, gotta, gotta, hear me.

Gotta hear me, gotta, gotta, hear me.

TOUR GUIDE TIP
Most children equate obedience with salvation. Take every opportunity to tell the children clearly that God wants us to obey his laws but sent Jesus to pay the penalty for our inevitable disobedience.

Items to Pack: safety helmet, and, for each child, 1 copy of the "Safety Gear? Never Fear!" handout (p. 17), scissors, glue, crayons, pen

TOUR GUIDE TIP
When the older children have finished, they can help the younger children cut out the safety gear. This accomplishes three things: It gives the older kids something constructive to do, it makes them feel useful, and it helps the younger kids complete their work with the group. Teach the older kids not to *do* the work for the younger kids but rather to help them with what they can't do on their own.

SCENIC ROUTE
Using a wipe-off crayon, write the point on the helmet: "God's loving laws keep us safe." Pass the helmet around for the children to read. (You can wipe off the crayon with a cloth or paper towel.)

ONE WAY

(15 minutes)
A-Maze-ing Grace

The children will follow an obstacle course to Christ.

Preparation: Cut out the stone tablets. Punch two holes at the top, and run yarn through them so they can be worn as a necklace. Use classroom furniture to set up a maze. The children can wander between rows of chairs and crawl under tunnels of tables.

Place a picture of Jesus at the end of the maze. Next to it, lay a piece of paper that reads, "God gave us loving laws to keep us safe. They lead us to Jesus."

Gather the kids and ask:

• **How many of you have obeyed all of God's commandments? How many of you have always obeyed your parents?**

• **Why did God give us laws if he knew we couldn't keep them?**

Say: **The Bible says, "The law was our schoolmaster to bring us unto Christ"** (Galatians 3:24a, King James Version). **A schoolmaster is someone who watches over your safety.**

Have the children work in teams of two. Child A will wear the Ten Commandments around his or her neck and will hold the hand of Child B, whose eyes will be closed. Child A will lead Child B safely through the maze to the picture of Jesus. Child A will read the paper that says, "God gave us loving laws to keep us safe. They lead us to Jesus." Give each child a chance to go through the maze.

Ask:

• **Where did your guide lead you?**

• **Why can't we get to God by keeping his laws?**

Read Galatians 3:24a again: **"The law was our schoolmaster to bring us unto Christ."**

Ask:

• **What does Jesus do when we come to him?**

Say: God gave us loving laws to keep us safe. His loving laws lead us to Jesus. **Only Jesus can forgive us for the times we do break God's laws.**

SCENIC ROUTE

Photocopy the "Stone Tablets" handout (p. 9) for each child in your class. The children can add the page to their notebooks or make their own Ten Commandments necklace.

HOME AGAIN PRAYER

(5 minutes)

Have ten children each write a different one of the Ten Commandments on a sheet of paper. Tape the papers to the backs of ten chairs, and have the children use the chairs to form a rectangular "fence." Talk about being protected by God's loving laws. Gather the children inside the fence for this closing prayer.

Dear God, thank you for your loving laws that keep us safe. Thank you for using them to lead us to Jesus. We ask your help in keeping your commandments. When we do fail, please forgive us. Thank you for choosing us as your special people. Amen.

Safety Gear? Never Fear!

God's Loving Laws Keep Me Safe.

You shall have no other gods before me.

Be true to your husband or wife.

You shall not want what others have.

Honor your father and mother.

You shall not kill.

You shall not lie.

You shall not steal.

You shall not make any idols.

Speak God's name with respect.

Set aside a special day for God.

The First Commandment:
You Shall Have No Other Gods Before Me

Pathway Point: 🌐 Worship God alone.

TOUR GUIDE TIP

Enlarge the first commandment on page 10, and make a copy for each child in your class. Have crayons or markers available so children arriving early or leaving late can color and decorate these pages for their notebooks.

TOUR GUIDE TIP

The activities in this book have been designed for multi-age groups. Select from the activities, or adapt them as needed for your class.

In-Focus Verse: "And God spoke all these words: 'I am the Lord your God, who brought you out of Egypt, out of the land of slavery. You shall have no other gods before me' " (Exodus 20:1-3).

Travel Itinerary

God established his authority with the children of Israel when he rescued them from the Egyptians. Coming out of Egypt, the Israelites must have considered monotheism (worshipping only one god) a rather radical concept. The Egyptians worshipped many deities, including Ra, the sun god; Horus, god of heaven; Shu, god of the air; and Nut, goddess of the sky. Out of the whirlwind of little gods, our God speaks, "I am the Lord your God...You shall have no other gods before me." Today we have temptations to worship God in other religions. In many social circles, the current buzzword is "tolerance." But Christianity was never meant to be a benevolent symposium of collective religious sympathy. Today gods can masquerade behind science, parapsychology, and multiculturalism, to name a few.

As this world shrinks and our kids bump into Buddhists, New Agers, and humanists, pantheism is being disguised as diversity. God doesn't stand for it. He says, "I am the Lord, and there is no other" (Isaiah 45:18b). This chapter seeks to equip our children with spiritual detectors as they walk through a new millennium of potential pitfalls. The children will discover that out of the profusion of beliefs, idols, and religious practices, God stands alone as worthy to be worshipped.

DEPARTURE PRAYER (5 minutes)

Too often, children's prayers are reduced to asking God for material things or for healing a friend. That's a good start. But teach the children to ask God for spiritual growth, too. Consider passing around a pair of glasses from which the lenses have been removed (you might ask your optometrist to lend you a pair) while the students pray for God to open their eyes.

Say: **Dear Lord, we shall have no other God but you. Please help us to** 🌐 **worship you alone. Help us, please, Lord, to open our eyes and ears for things, people, and ideas that steal your place as God. Help us be brave enough to stand up for you. Thank you for helping us obey you. Amen.**

1st STOP DISCOVERY (15 minutes)
Green—Go, Yellow—Slow

This game teaches the children to think carefully about different situations so they will worship God alone.

Give each child an index card. Ask him or her to draw a rectangle and to write the first commandment around the outside of the rectangle: "You shall have no other gods before me." Younger kids can copy from the board, "Worship God alone."

Stand in the front of the room. Place the sheets of colored dots in separate piles according to color near you. Open your Bible to Exodus 20:3 and say: **God's first commandment says, "You shall have no other gods before me." Other gods come in so many forms that sometimes we don't recognize them. We'll discover how to be sure we** 🕐 **worship God alone.**

Your index card will be your traffic signal. I'll read a situation to you, and you will decide what to do in that situation. If what I read to you helps you worship God alone, then it is like a green light. Come up here and get a green sticker to put on your traffic signal card, and then return to your place. If something besides God is being worshipped, do not move, but raise your card. I will bring you a red sticker to add to your card. If it's a situation in which you are not sure if it is God alone being worshipped, walk slowly up here and put a yellow sticker on your card. You can layer your stickers.

Here's the first situation.

• **Your friend plays a CD. You like the music. When you listen to the words, they are praising God.** The children should come up and get a green sticker.

Read aloud Psalm 149:3.

• **In studying about American Indians, you learned about the shamans, or medicine men. Your teacher asks you to make a drum to beat while a medicine man chants to cure a sickness.** The children should hold up their cards. Give each child a red sticker.

Read aloud Exodus 15:26.

• **You are swimming in your Muslim friend's new pool, telling her how great it is. She says her family praises Allah for it.** The children should come up to get a yellow sticker.

Read aloud Deuteronomy 4:39.

• **You are at a slumber party. After midnight the kids gather around a candle to talk to ghosts.** Give each child a red sticker.

Read aloud Deuteronomy 18:12.

• **The movie you've just seen was awesome. The hero, a little boy, was called the Chosen One and had the power of the Force.** The children should come up to get a yellow sticker.

Read aloud Matthew 12:18.

• **Your gym teacher is making you run a mile, and you aren't sure you can finish. You ask your grandma in heaven to give you the strength to finish.** The children should hold up their cards. Give each child a red sticker.

Read aloud Isaiah 8:19.

• **Just for fun, you let your cousin read your horoscope for today.** The children should come up to get a yellow sticker.

Read aloud Isaiah 47:13.

Items to Pack: package of red, green, and yellow sticker dots, and, for each child, index card, pen (If you can't find the stickers, let your kids draw circles on their cards and color them in with crayons.)

SCENIC ROUTE → Make your own stoplight that will really stop kids in their tracks. Paint a box black, and cut out three large circles in a vertical row. Cover one circle with red cellophane, one with yellow, and one with green. Shine a flashlight behind the correct color.

TOUR GUIDE TIP This game will inevitably raise important questions. Write down any questions the children ask, and be sure to address them after the game. Use this opportunity to teach the children about the fine line Christians walk in obedience to Jesus—to be in the world but not of the world (John 17:16). Be sure to read your kids the full version of this commandment from your Bible.

• **Some kids are getting together for Easter. They want to have an egg hunt and read a story about Jesus rising from the dead.** The children should come up for a green sticker.

Read aloud Hebrews 10:25.

• **For Celebrate Mother Earth Day, you're supposed to hang a ribbon on a tree in her honor.** The children should hold up their cards. Give each one a red sticker.

Read aloud Exodus 20:3-5.

• **Your class is studying the gods of ancient Egypt. Some kids think it's cool that the Egyptians believed a cat was a god.** The children should hold up their cards. Give each one a red sticker.

Read aloud Isaiah 19:1.

Have the kids form pairs to discuss the following questions:

• **What are some situations in which something besides God was worshipped?**

• **Have you ever been in a situation like that?**

• **What can you do the next time you feel trapped in one of these situations?**

Say: God is serious about asking us to ◔ worship him alone. Be careful, little flock. Choices like the ones we've just practiced will come up. God chose you to be his special treasures and to worship only him.

STORY EXCURSION (15 minutes)
Jessica Stands Up

Read the true story on pages 25-26 to the class. If God alone is worshipped, children will quietly wave green paper. If God is not exactly being worshipped alone, they will wave yellow paper. If God is definitely not worshipped alone, the kids will wave red paper.

After the story, have the kids form pairs or trios and answer the following questions:

• **Has anyone ever asked you to worship something that isn't God?**

• **What would you have done if you had been Jessica?**

• **Do you know people who may not worship God alone? What can you do when you are invited to their homes?**

Say: Jessica did a brave thing. It isn't easy to stand up for God. Like Jessica, we need to ◔ worship God alone. As God's special and treasured people, we need to ask him to open our eyes and ears. He will help us to obey his law: "You shall have no other gods before me."

ADVENTURE IN LIVING GOD'S LAWS (10 minutes)
Stand-Up Rhyme

Say: We need to love and respect every person, but we don't need to accept what they believe if it goes against the Bible. God said, "I am the Lord, and there is no other" (Isaiah 45:5a). Don't ever be ashamed to stand up for God. Lead the kids in the following rhyme, indicating to them when they should sit and stand. Hold up colored paper as mentioned as you say the poem. Repeat the poem, having the children hold up the colored papers from the previous story.

TOUR GUIDE TIP

Give the children plenty of time to share their experiences. Prompt them with questions such as, "Have you ever felt uncomfortable about something you were asked to do?" The more children verbalize for themselves, the more their own discoveries will become indelibly impressed upon their minds and hearts. This is how they form their own Christlike values.

(Children sitting) **Green is for go. They're worshipping God.**

Yellow means slow. It's sounding odd.

Red means stop. It's not OK.

Have no other gods that get in the way.

(Have children stand up.) **Stand up for God! Don't be shy.**

Stand up for God! And hold your head high.

Should we worship God or Jesus? That's what some children will wonder. Take the time to point out that when we worship God, we are worshipping a being whose essence is expressed in three persons: the Father, the Son, and the Holy Spirit. See Colossians 1:15-20.

(15 minutes)
Role-Playing

Let the kids act out situations they might encounter in the real world.

Form teams of four or five children. Be sure to include older and younger kids on the same team. Give each team a dilemma in which they are faced with the choice of whether or not they will worship God alone. You can use the scenarios from the Green—Go, Yellow—Slow opening activity on page 18, or the kids can think of their own. Ask teams to each make up a three-minute skit incorporating the commandment, "You shall have no other gods before me." After time to practice, have each team present its skit to the rest of the class. Following is an example of a simple skit.

Sarah: Hey, Allysa, I hope you'll come to my slumber party.

Allysa: Friday night, right? I'm counting on it.

Sarah: Good. We're going to light candles and play Mary Worth.

Allysa: What's that?

Sarah: Don't you know? We try to bring the dead back and speak to them.

Allysa: You mean it's like praying to a ghost?

Sarah: Yeah, well, it's really just for fun. We don't really believe it.

Allysa: I hope not. The Bible says, "You shall have no other gods before me." That means if you're going to pray to anyone else, I couldn't join you.

Sarah: Hmmm. I guess that is like praying to a fake god.

Allysa: I got a new Pop Rock Boys video. What if I bring that and some popcorn?

Sarah: Sure. I guess Mary Worth is a pretty silly game anyway.

SOUVENIRS → (15 minutes)
A God Who Stands Out

With the help of crayons and markers, the children will make their God stand out alone.

Items to Pack: for each child, 1 copy of the "A God Who Stands Out" handout (p. 27) on white paper, white crayon, washable marker, cup of water

Say: **Our God stands out from all the gods people worship, even though he's invisible. Using a white crayon, write the following in the blank spaces on your paper: "I am the Lord your God."** Write the words on a board for children to copy. The younger kids can simply write "God" on their papers.

We can't see God, just as we can't see these words. But we know that he is real and stands out from other gods. As I read the names of other gods that may cry out for your love, time, and attention, dip your marker in water and "paint" over the

white words you wrote. Tell the kids that people made up false religions and gods so that they could feel, touch, and see them, but that our God is the one who created the fingers we have to feel, the ears we have to hear, and the eyes we have to see. We need to worship the Creator, and not something created. They'll enjoy watching their God "appear."

TRAVEL-ALONG COMMANDMENT SONG (5 minutes)

Teach the kids the following words and motions to the second stanza of the "Travel-Along Commandment Song." Then have the children sing both stanzas they've learned and the refrain. (See pages 6-8.) This song serves as a review each week and a powerful way to impress God's laws into their minds and hearts.

"I am the Lord, your God," says he. *(Point finger up.)*
"You shall have no other gods but *me*! *(Point to self.)*
Worship God and God alone. *(Put hands together and bow.)*
You're his flock, his very own." *(Hug self.)*

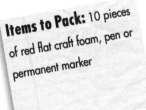

Items to Pack: 10 pieces of red flat craft foam, pen or permanent marker

ONE WAY ▷ (10 minutes) Crisis to the Cross

Use foam pieces to help kids think about the commandments and whether or not they can keep the commandments.

Preparation: Write one of the Ten Commandments on each of the ten pieces of foam. (See pages 9-10 for a simply worded version of the commandments.) A staircase would help to illustrate the point, but if one is not available, spread the foam pieces on the ground and compare them to steppingstones.

Gather the children and say: **A lot of people think that the way to God is to keep all of his commandments. Let's see how well we keep them.** Place the sixth commandment on the first step, and say: **If you have never killed anyone, you may stand on this step.** After the kids have responded, place the second commandment on the second step. **If you have never made any idols, climb to step two. Very good.**

Continue this way, from the easiest commandments to obey to the toughest—the eighth, third, fourth, tenth, first, ninth, and fifth. When you reach the fifth, it is unlikely that anyone will be on that step. Read Romans 3:23.

Say: **Does this mean our situation is hopeless? No! Not at all.** Read Romans 7:24-25 and Hebrews 9:15. Then gather the ten foam pieces, and turn them over on the floor, shaping them into a cross—six down and four across.

Say: **God uses his laws to show us our sin. This brings us to Jesus. At the cross of Jesus we say, "Help! I can't do this!" And he will help us. His death on the cross paid for your sins. That's the kind of God we have—the only one worth worshipping!**

HOME AGAIN PRAYER

(5 minutes)

Have the kids sit down. Give them each a turn to say this prayer. When they come to the words, "I will stand up..." have them stand up and continue the prayer.

Dear Lord, you alone are to be worshipped. Help me to never worship anyone or anything but you. Help me to know when I should stop and go and proceed slowly. Give me the strength and courage to *stand* up for you. I praise you because you are the one true God. Amen.

(10 minutes)

Sand Scratchings

People want to write! Since early history, people have found some way to record their impressions. Whether it's painting on a cave wall, carving images into ivory, or typing on a computer keyboard, people want to make their thoughts visible.

One of the earliest and crudest forms of writing a message was scratching it into sand. Even today, children love to write in sand. In this activity, you will help children write the first commandment as a sand print. You may want to shorten the wording to "You shall have no other gods," or for younger kids, "No other gods."

1. Lay the paper on newspaper, and spray the paper with the spray glue or use a glue stick. Cover the entire paper.

2. Sprinkle sand all over the paper, and shake off the excess.

3. Scratch the commandment in with a craft stick.

4. Spray the whole paper with clear acrylic coating for permanency.

Did You Know?

Just about anything and everything has been used as a surface to write on. Before paper was invented, people wrote on animal skins, clay, silk, bamboo strips, rags, and even potatoes. Look around you. What types of surfaces do we use inside and outside to print our messages on today?

FUN FACT

For a lot of reasons, writing in sand isn't a smart way to keep messages. You can't carry the message from one place to another. One strong wave or gust of wind could wipe out your words. Animal footprints could destroy your message. But nothing can stop man from inventing new ways of taking ideas from the mind and recording them for all the world to see! Aren't you glad about that?

FUN FACT

Man has even used leaves to write on. In fact, we sometimes call the pages of a book "leaves." Some people in Italy cut a tree open and made the inner bark into a type of paper. The trees were called liber trees. Our word "library" comes from this word.

Jessica Stands Up

Jessica raced ahead of Emily to her Kids Around the World Club.

"Hurry up, Emily," Jessica said. "We're going to make Chinese kites." Jessica loved the crafts, songs, and games they played to explore the world.

Jessica was the first one there. Miss Taken was pulling a strange statue out of a closet.

"What's that?" Jessica asked.

Miss Taken spun around, "Oh, Jess, let me introduce you to Buddha." Children wave yellow papers. The gold statue was of a fat man wearing robes. He was sitting with his legs crossed. His head was down, and he seemed to be concentrating. Miss Taken placed the statue in the center of a table in the middle of the room. As the other kids arrived, she carefully placed some artificial flowers around the statue. Children continue to wave yellow papers.

Then Miss Taken said to the group, "Children, remember that we've been studying Eastern countries. Today we're going to make kites for Buddha, who is an important part of one of the religions in that area." Children wave red papers.

Jessica suddenly remembered what she had learned about God's commandments: "Worship God alone." Children wave green papers. Jessica squirmed. Her stomach did flip-flops. Miss Taken had the group make kites out of rice paper and decorate them. Jessica whispered to Emily, "I'm not sure about all this. Children wave yellow papers. I mean what about the commandment that says, "You shall have no other gods"? Children wave green papers.

"Lighten up, Jessica," Emily said.

"But you sat right next to me in Sunday school when we learned the first commandment." Children wave green papers.

"We're not bowing down," said Emily. "Can I borrow your marker?"

The other kids were busy decorating their kites with stickers while Miss Taken said, "At our festival, we'll lay the kites at Buddha's feet in honor of the wonderful year we've had." Children wave red papers. "We'll be inviting our parents and grandparents." Miss Taken continued talking about the festival.

Jessica hardly heard Miss Taken because her head seemed to be swimming with the words she had learned in church that week: "You shall have no other gods before me. Worship God alone." Children wave green papers.

"Jessica," Miss Taken said, "the other kids are finished. Please, hurry."

"Miss Taken, I...I...I need some stickers." Jessica wished she weren't so shy. She wanted to tell her teacher how she felt. Children wave yellow papers.

The kids were gathering around the statue as Miss Taken explained that many people around the world honor Buddha—people who live in countries such as Japan, India, China, and even here in the United States. Jessica thought, "It's OK to learn about other religions. But if she asks me to honor him, that would be putting a god before my God." Children wave green papers. Jessica listened closely to her teacher while she dipped her marker in water and swirled colors on her kite.

Miss Taken said, "I'll teach you a song to sing while we are laying our gifts at Buddha's feet." Children wave red papers.

Jessica stood up. The kite and markers tumbled to the ground. Jessica took a big breath and said, "Miss Taken, I won't be at the festival."

"Oh, too bad, Jessica. Are you going out of town?"

"No. If I came, I would be breaking God's first commandment that says, 'You shall have no other gods before me.' I can't be a part of that." Children wave green papers.

The room got very quiet. Everyone's eyes seemed to be like lasers shooting through Jessica.

"Oh," Miss Taken said. "I see."

Emily stood up next and said, "I won't be there either." Children continue to wave green papers.

Then Jake stood up. Children continue to wave green papers. Then Miguel. Children continue to wave green papers. Jessica said, "Miss Taken, I enjoy learning about other countries and religions. But when you ask us to make gifts and honor something that isn't God, it goes against God's laws about worshipping him alone."

"Well, I never really thought of it like that," Miss Taken said. "Of course, I'd never ask you to do something you don't feel right about."

Jessica was glad that she had stood up for God.

A God Who Stands Out

Buddha

horoscopes

sun worship

zodiac signs

pyramids

mother earth

praying to angels

crystals

fire god

The Second Commandment: You Shall Not Make Any Idols

Pathway Point: 🌑 God wants and deserves first place in your life.

TOUR GUIDE TIP

Enlarge the second commandment on page 10, and make a copy for each child in your class. Have crayons or markers available so children arriving early or leaving late can color and decorate the pages for their notebooks.

TOUR GUIDE TIP

The activities in this book have been designed for multi-age groups. Select from the activities or adapt them as needed for your class.

TOUR GUIDE TIP

Define "idol" and "idolatry" for your kids as any created person or thing that takes the place of God. On their commandment page, have children write the correct definition. (Kindergarten kids may need to have the word "created" defined as "what is made." They may understand the word "idol" best as a "fake god.")

In-Focus Verse: "You shall not make for yourself an idol in the form of anything in heaven above or on the earth beneath or in the waters below. You shall not bow down to them or worship them; for I, the Lord your God, am a jealous God" (Exodus 20:4).

Travel Itinerary

The Israelites journeyed through lands of many idols. This was akin to walking through a dangerous minefield. God instituted the second commandment as a pathway to safety: "You shall not make for yourself an idol." Our idols are less obvious today. They come in the form of things that sneak into our lives to grab our time and affection. What is your idol? Is it position? your children? your job? your house? Whatever contends with God can become an idol. Let God be your God, not other things.

God wants first place in our lives. Even children have temptations that pull them away from God. This lesson will practically help children identify the things that compete with God as the premier love in life. They will learn that the commandments are not given from a vain god on an ego trip. The commandments are from our God who is the only one who deserves first place in our hearts and lives.

DEPARTURE PRAYER (5 minutes)

As you say this prayer, pause to let your students take turns thanking God for his blessings.

Say: **Dear Lord, our God, thank you for all the wonderful things in this world that you have given us to enjoy, such as** [pause as children name specific blessings]. **Sometimes we let these things take first place in our hearts. Help us to understand what it means to put you first in our hearts. Show us the things in our lives that sneak in as idols. Show us what we need to take out of our lives so that we can put more of you in. Help us so that we have no other gods before you. Amen.**

1ˢᵗ STOP DISCOVERY (10 minutes)
No Room for God

This wet-but-wonderful activity illustrates how a heart crowded with worldly things removes God from first place in our lives.

Preparation: Pour a cup of water for each child.

Hand each child a rock and a marker. Ask the children to think about what takes up a lot of their time, attention, and money—for example, TV, video or computer games, soccer

Items to Pack: plastic bucket or pitcher (be sure the container holds as many cups of water as there are children in the class), water, tray, and, for each child, cup, rock, red permanent marker

practice, or playing with friends. Have the children write or draw those things on their rocks. Use a red permanent marker to draw several large hearts on the pitcher, and place the pitcher on the tray. Hand each child a cup of water.

Say: **This pitcher is like an empty heart. Let's fill this heart with God. When it's your turn, pour water into the pitcher and say, "God deserves first place in my heart because..." Then tell us something about who God is. For example, as I pour my water in, I'll say, "God deserves first place in my heart because he is my** *creator*."

Let each child have a turn until the pitcher is nearly full. Check out the following passages for more of God's qualities: Psalm 104:24 and Proverbs 3:19.

Say: **Our hearts are full of the goodness of God, but sometimes other things try to crowd into our hearts. Each of you may now tell us what's drawn on your rock and then place your rock into the water.** As the children add their rocks, the water will overflow. When they have finished, ask:

• **What happened to the water? Why?**

• **How is this like what happens in our own hearts with God?**

• **How can we keep our hearts full of God so he has first place?**

Say: God's second commandment is "You shall not make any idols." Sometimes things we love become like idols, crowding God out. 🌀 But God wants and deserves first place in your life.

STORY EXCURSION / (15 minutes)
Baseball or God?

Hand out the "Baseball or God?" skit (pages 35-36) about a young boy who goes through a whole day without God. Have the "angels" read the skit while "Joshua" acts out the motions.

Say: **In the second commandment God said, "You shall not make for yourself an idol...You shall not bow down to them or worship them; for I, the Lord your God, am a jealous God" (Exodus 20:4). That means that** 🌀 **God wants and deserves first place in your heart. When other things try to steal God's place, we can think of them as idols. God is serious about wanting first place in our hearts.**

Select two children to read the angels' lines and a third to act out Joshua's role. Before you tell the children to begin the skit, say: **Let's see if Joshua will put God first today with his time, thoughts, prayers, money, and love.**

After the skit, ask:

• **What place do you think God has in Joshua's life? Why?**

• **How are you like Joshua?**

• **How can you give God first place in your heart?**

Say: **God's second commandment is "You shall have no idols." God knows that other things try to steal his place. These things become like idols to us. God won't settle for number two.** 🌀 **He wants and deserves first place in your life. Won't you make room for him today?**

Items to Pack: copies of the "Baseball or God?" script (pp. 35-36), simple props for the 2 angels (such as gold chenille wires fashioned into halos), baseball bat, timer that rings

TOUR GUIDE TIP When you ask questions, give the kids plenty of time to answer. Don't hurry to the next point or activity. When children speak their minds, the lesson becomes their own, and that is exactly what you are trying to accomplish. When "nontalkers" speak up—let them talk. They will feel more a part of the class and, thus, more a part of the church.

TOUR GUIDE TIP

If you have fewer than twelve children in your class, have them move to open chairs after their first turn.

SCENIC ROUTE →

As a follow-up to this game, let the kids make their own clocks out of paper plates and brass fasteners. Have the children each write on the outside perimeter, "You shall not make any idols." On the arms of the clock, they can write, "All day long I have held out my hands" (Isaiah 65:2). Let the clock serve as a reminder that God is ready and waiting to have first place in their lives.

ADVENTURE IN LIVING GOD'S LAWS

(10 minutes)
All Day Long

In this activity, the children will move from chair to chair to represent a clock.

Preparation: Position twelve chairs in a circle, with each chair facing the center of the circle. Put a chair in the middle for yourself, preferably a chair that you can spin around on. Write the numerals one through twelve on separate sheets of paper, and tape each sheet to a chair back.

Say: God said, "You shall not make any idols."  God wants and deserves first place in your life. But we get so busy, don't we? Sometimes a whole day can slip by, without us giving God any of our time or love. God said, "I said, 'Here am I, here am I.' All day long I have held out my hands to an obstinate people." (Isaiah 65:1-2). Let's pretend that I am God. I'll sit here with my arms outstretched, like the arms of a clock. Each of you will sit on a chair and tell me what you do each day at the time marked on the back of your chair.

Choose twelve children to sit on the chairs. If you do not have twelve children, fill in as many of the chairs as you can. If you have a larger class, the other kids will stand behind the chairs, waiting for their turns. Sitting on the chair in the middle, say: "Here I am! I want and deserve first place in your life!" and point to a child. Have the child tell you what he or she does at the time designated on his or her chair.

Continue in this manner until you have been around the circle once. Then encourage the kids to come to you for a hug while you remind them that God wants first place in their lives. If some children are standing, have them trade places with those sitting. Repeat the activity, but this time have children state different ways they can include God in their day. For example, the child sitting at 6:00 might say, "I will thank God for my supper before I eat."

To conclude the activity, have the kids find an honesty partner (one they can be honest with) and discuss the following question:

• **What things can steal God's place in my life?**

SOUVENIRS →

(10 minutes)
First-Place Race

The children will mark a chart with candy to determine who has first place in their lives.

Preparation: Give each child some M&M's to use as markers for the following exercise. Then the children can take their charts home to fill in daily with colored pencils or markers.

Say: We all love certain people and things. But these can become like idols. As God's special people, we want to obey God when he says, "You shall not make any idols." We're going to determine what it could be that is winning first place in our lives. Look on the bottom of the left-hand column on your chart. "God" is written there. In the empty spaces in that column, write things or people that you love or things you love to do. For example, you might fill in the blank spaces with "my trophy collection," "in-line skating," or "my best friend."

When the kids have finished, explain that they will fill in the appropriate squares with candy as they answer your questions. Have the older kids help the younger ones to fill in the chart.

Ask:

- **Who or what takes up most of your time every day?**
- **Who or what takes up most of your energy?**
- **Who or what takes up most of your thoughts?**
- **Who or what takes up most of your money?**
- **Who or what takes up most of your love?**

Say: **In the "Total" column, add up the number of candies in each row.**

Ask:

- **Which one won?**

Say: **God gave us the second commandment as a reminder: "You shall not make any idols." Watch out for those people or things that want to grab first place from God. Only God deserves first place in your life. When God is the winner, you'll be a winner!**

(15 minutes)
Our Capital G God

Play this game to compare our God to the material gods that can't fulfill us.

Items to Pack: chalk-board and chalk or marker board and markers

Write the letters "od" all over the board with a blank in front of each for the kids to fill in the first letter. Have the children form two teams.

Say: **Things we love can sneak in and become idols. Idols are little gods. If you ever see the word "god" with a lowercase "g," it means a fake god, not the Lord our God. When you see the word "God" with a capital G, it means the real true God.** (Write both a capital G and a lowercase "g" on the board.)

Hand a marker to the first child on each team. Tell the teams that you will tell them a quality of a god. If it is a quality of a fake god, they should find a place to add a lowercase "g" to one of the blanks. If it is a quality of the one true God, they should add a capital G to one of the blanks. Randomly describe either a quality of fake gods or of the one true God. After the description, the first kids from each team will run up to the board and fill in either a capital G or a lowercase "g." They will pass off the markers to the next kids in line, who will do the same for the next quality. Continue until all kids have had a chance to go to the board. After the game, give kids a chance to come up with their own qualities of both.

Following are some examples:

Our capital G God...

- can fill your heart with true joy.
- forgives sin.
- is able to heal.
- is perfectly holy.
- knows your every thought.
- loves you.
- hears everyone in the world at the same time.

Little "g" fake gods…

• can not make you happy.

• can change.

• will crumble into dust.

• can be carried around.

• are expensive.

• can't love you.

Say: **Isn't it odd that people would settle for a little god?**

Travel-Along Commandment Song
(5 minutes)

TRAVEL-ALONG COMMANDMENT SONG

Teach your kids the following lines and accompanying motions for the third stanza of the "Travel-Along Commandment Song." See pages 6-8 to review all the stanzas learned previously.

You shall not make an idol is commandment number two *(hold up right index finger, then left),*
'Cause second place for God won't do. *(Cross fingers in an X.)*
God wants first place in your life and heart. *(Hold up one finger; point it to your heart.)*
That's the way to live—that's really smart! *(Tap your temple.)*

Items to Pack: flashlight, 10 pennies

ONE WAY

Sit in darkness. Use a flashlight to read Romans 1:21-23 from *The Living Bible*:

"Yes, they knew about him all right, but they wouldn't admit it or worship him or even thank him for all his daily care. And after awhile they began to think up silly ideas of what God was like and what he wanted them to do. The result was that their foolish minds became dark and confused. Claiming themselves to be wise without God, they became utter fools instead. And then, instead of worshiping the glorious, ever-living God, they took wood and stone and made idols for themselves, carving them to look like mere birds and animals and snakes and puny men."

Talk about the darkness that people live in all over the world. Mention how sad it is that only 20 percent of the people on earth are Christian. Explain what 20 percent means by having ten children come up to the front and each hold one of the pennies. Have two children remain standing while eight sit down. (Warn younger kids about not putting coins in their mouth.)

Say: **But Jesus broke through the darkness.** Turn the lights on. Have an older child read John 12:46-47. Have the kids share reasons why Jesus is the light of the world.

(5 minutes)

As children pray, have each child take a rock out of the bucket (from the opening activity) and name what is written on it.

Dear Lord, thank you for being a God that deserves first place in our lives and hearts. Lord, sometimes it's hard to know what is taking your place. We're sorry for the times we've let [have kids name what's written on their rocks] **fill up our hearts and crowd you out. Remind us when that is happening. Thank you for sending Jesus to die on the cross. As much as we'd like to, we can't always obey. So thank you, dear Jesus, for paying the price for our sin. Amen.**

BACK ROAD TO WRITING

(10 minutes)
Written on Rock

When God handed Moses the Ten Commandments, they were actually engraved by the finger of God. We can't replicate that, but we can produce a surface that looks like a rock. Making images in rock was one of the early ways people recorded their thoughts. You'll need extra adult helpers for this craft.

Preparation: Make a sample of the stone tablet at least a day before class, allowing time for it to harden.

1. Form a rectangle or "tablet" mold out of foil, making sure the lip of the mold is at least one inch high.

2. Mix the plaster of Paris according to the package instructions.

3. Pour the plaster into the foil mold, making sure it is flat enough for a writing surface about ¼ inch thick so it will not crack when dry.

4. Allow the plaster to harden. The time factor will vary according to the room's humidity, the plaster's brand, and the thickness of the tablet.

5. When the plaster has completely hardened, give it a gray, rockish color by scribbling all over it with a pencil. Then smear the pencil marks with a paper towel.

6. Use a permanent marker to write the commandment.

7. *Mazel tov!* You have completed your second commandment!

FUN FACT The Old Testament was written in Hebrew. Hebrew is read from right to left, the opposite of what we are used to. If you opened a book at the last chapter and skimmed through the pages backward to the first chapter, you would be reading a book as those reading Hebrew do.

Did You Know?

Did you know that the Ten Commandments were engraved on both the front and back surfaces? Moses smashed the first set on the ground, but God never scolded him for doing so. The second set of tablets was placed in a special box called the ark of the covenant. The tablets were lost many years ago, and their whereabouts remains a mystery.

Did You Know?

Did you know that the Hebrew Scriptures were originally written without any vowels? In the Hebrew Scriptures, the word "Yahweh" (their word for "Lord") appears almost seven thousand times as YHWH. We guess at which letters to add as vowels to form the word "Yahweh."

Extra Cool

You can make two large tablets, write five commandments on each one, and stick a paper clip "hanger" in the back of each tablet before it hardens. You can make your commandment extra cool by writing a real Hebrew word on your tablet. The Hebrew word for "commandments" is "mitzvot." (See the margin to see how it looks in Hebrew.)

Baseball or God?

(Timer rings.)

Angel 1: Ah! Monday morning! Joshua is getting up. *(Louder)* Joshua is getting up! He's rubbing the sleep out of his eyes and moaning as he looks at the clock.

Angel 2: I know he'll say his morning prayers. I know it! I know it! *(Addressing the kids)* Don't you think he will?

Angel 1: Don't hold your breath. Nope. There he goes, slurping down his cereal without thanking God for his food.

Angel 2: Oh, I'm so embarrassed! Just wait, though. He'll read his Bible while he's waiting for the bus. Joshua does want God to have first place in his life.

Angel 1: I don't think so—he's pulling his "Baseball Is My Life" magazine out of his backpack.

Angel 2: *(Covering his eyes)* Oh, no, I hate even the name of that magazine. It goes against God's second command, "You shall not make any idols."

Angel 1: The kids don't understand that!

Angel 2: *(Addressing the kids)* Hey, you kids can understand that when you put other things in your life, they become like idols, can't you? *(To Angel 1)* Give them some credit!

Angel 1: Hey, perk up! Joshua will be getting his test back today.

Angel 2: I remember that he prayed really hard for help with that one. He'll probably thank God when he gets a good grade.

Angel 1: Yeah, sure. *(Addressing the kids)* Do you think he'll thank God?

Angel 2: Listen, those kids are talking about a baseball game tonight. They're inviting Joshua! Hey, they don't play on Wednesday nights!

Angel 1: Tonight they will. Remember the rain last week?

Angel 2: Well, Joshua won't go. He loves going to church on Wednesdays. And tonight is awards night...*No!* Joshua, how could you?

Angel 1: I wonder how that makes God feel. Must be tough always having to take second place.

Angel 2: It's more like fifth place in Joshua's life.

(Angels shake their heads and sigh.)

Angel 1: Hey, Joshua's getting his test back. It's...an A!

Angel 2: Get ready and open those ears! We're gonna hear some thank yous now!

(They put hands by their ears and wait and wait and wait.)

Angel 1: I see a lot of high fives. *(Addressing the kids)* Do you think Joshua will say thank you to God?

Angel 2: I see a proud smile on Joshua's face.

(Angels sigh and shake their heads.)

Angel 1: At least Joshua brought his money to school. He's going to give it to the poor kids from Haiti.

Angel 2: That's my boy! He thought of that all on his own. Boy, was I proud when he decided to put God first in his life by giving those kids his money!

Angel 1: *(Covering the eyes of Angel 2)* Never mind. You don't want to see it!

Angel 2: *(Struggling against him)* I can take it!

Angel 1: It's not you he's hurting. I'm worried about what this will do to his love for God.

Angel 2: He didn't...He did. Joshua gave that money to Chris for more baseball cards!

Angel 1: Wow, you'd think that Joshua never learned the commandment "You shall not make any idols."

Angel 2: Come on, let's watch this ballgame.

Angel 1: Look at that! The bases are loaded, and Joshua is up. Yes! He's doing it! He's praying to God, asking him for help!

Angel 2: It's about time.

(Joshua swings his bat.)

Angel 1: Oh, he missed. Bummer, he missed again. But at least he's praying!

Angel 2: Whoopee. Some time to put God first in your life, when you need a grand...

Angel 1: *(Jumping up and down)* Yahoo! A grand slam! Look at that kid go! That's my boy. I'm gonna sit right here and watch those thanks rise up to God like smoke drifting up from a barbecue! Mmm. I can't wait to see God smile! *(Addressing the kids)* Now do you think Joshua will thank God? *(Pause.)* I'm waiting. And waiting. And waiting.

Angel 2: I give up. I think I'll go back to rescuing kids from broken bones.

Angel 1: *(Covering face and sobbing)* I can't stand it! God wants and deserves first place in our lives, and he doesn't even get a thank you for a grand slam!

Angel 2: *(Puts an arm around Angel 1 as they walk off together.)* Instead of being a guardian angel, maybe I'd better become a "teach-ian" angel and teach the kids what it means to have no idols, like baseball, in their lives.

Angel 1: Yeah, let's get a hot dog while we talk about it.

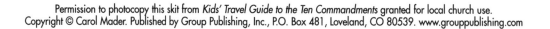

First-Place Race

GOD WANTS AND DESERVES FIRST PLACE

What You Love	Monday	Tuesday	Wednesday	Thursday	Friday	Saturday	Sunday	Total
GOD								

"I AM THE LORD YOUR GOD."

GOD WANTS AND DESERVES FIRST PLACE IN YOUR LIFE.

"YOU SHALL NOT HAVE ANY IDOLS."

JOURNEY 4

The Third Commandment:
Speak God's Name With Respect

Pathway Point: ● Our words tell what's in our hearts.

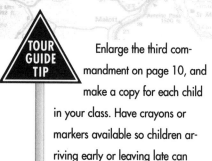

TOUR GUIDE TIP
Enlarge the third commandment on page 10, and make a copy for each child in your class. Have crayons or markers available so children arriving early or leaving late can color and decorate the pages for their notebooks.

TOUR GUIDE TIP
The activities in this book have been designed for multi-age groups. Select from the activities or adapt them as needed for your class.

TOUR GUIDE TIP
In this book we have interpreted God's commandments so that even young children can understand them, but we don't want to rob the kids of the scriptural wording of the Ten Commandments. Some kids may even have memorized a different version of the commandments. Encourage the kids to check out different Bible translations, and ask children how they would write the commandments in their own words.

Items to Pack: different items that relate to a person's work—1 item and 1 piece of paper for each child in your class—plus 2 extra pieces of paper, putty or masking tape, pens

In-Focus Verse: "You shall not misuse the name of the Lord your God, for the Lord will not hold anyone guiltless who misuses his name" (Exodus 20:7).

Travel Itinerary

Think of the screeching, nauseating sound of fingernails scraping down a chalkboard. Ouch, it hurts the ears! It should be the same for us when someone takes God's name in vain. God is not unaware of our words. He says, "All day long my name is constantly blasphemed" (Isaiah 52:5b). When one Bible teacher mentioned Jesus Christ, a little girl exclaimed, "You said a swear word!" How God's heart must break when his name is no longer connected to his loving character.

Our children would have to be deaf to avoid the vulgar and blasphemous expletives gushing from TV, our neighbors, and even our schools. This lesson focuses on the fact that our speech reflects the condition of our hearts. A transformed heart will result in transformed speech. Respect for God and God's name begins with a humbled heart.

DEPARTURE PRAYER (5 minutes)

When Jesus taught us to pray, he gave priority to speaking God's name with respect. Matthew 6:9 says, "This, then, is how you should pray: 'Our Father in heaven, hallowed be your name.' " Hallowed means to make holy or to set apart. Have your kids look up Matthew 6:9 and tell you other ways to address God with respect. One suggestion would be to bow or salute.

Say: **Dear Father in heaven, you are wonderful. Your name is wonderful. We honor you by honoring your name. Please teach us to speak your name with respect. Everything you are is wrapped up in your name.** ● **Our words tell what's in our hearts. Let our words come from hearts that love you. Help us so that we never misuse your name. Amen.**

1st STOP DISCOVERY (15 minutes)
Word Clues

In this fun matching game, the kids will learn that their words reflect who they are.

Preparation: Cut each piece of paper to form a balloon, like the word balloons in cartoon strips. Write words that reflect a different person's profession in each balloon. Include some trade jargon, but don't make it too difficult. You will need a corresponding item for each word balloon. For example, for a photographer, you might write, "Set the shutter speed for my next picture." The corresponding item could be a roll of film. For a carpenter, you might write: "I think I will need sixteen penny nails to frame up this wall." Use a hammer for the corresponding item. Write on one extra piece of paper: "@#%, I'm angry!" Write on another speech balloon, "Dear God, please help me to speak your name with respect." Hang the word balloons around the room and pile the corresponding items in the center of the room.

Say: **Our words tell who we are. Let's find out who would speak the words in the speech bubbles posted on the walls.**

Have the kids line up at one end of the room. Read the first word bubble. Let the kids search items and search for the item that corresponds to the words. Tell kids that whoever finds the correct item first will walk to the word bubble and state the occupation. Continue until all the occupations have been named. All of the kids will be standing under one word bubble. Say **Just as the words you are standing under helped you know what type of person said the words, so these last two word bubbles can give you clues to know what kind of person said them.** Read the sign that says, "@#%, I'm angry!" Explain that this means someone spoke God's name without respect, as an expression of anger.

Ask:

• **What type of a person would speak like that?**

• **How do these words tell what's inside this person's heart?**

Read the sign that says, "Dear God, please help me to speak your name with respect."

Ask:

• **What type of a person would speak like that?**

• **How do these words tell what's inside this person's heart?**

Our words are like clues, telling the whole world what's in our hearts. That's why God gave us the third commandment: "You shall not misuse the name of the Lord your God, for the Lord will not hold anyone guiltless who misuses his name." God is serious when he tells us to speak his name with respect.

STORY EXCURSION (15 minutes)
Words as Windows

In this activity, the children will share in the telling of this story. It includes an invitation to follow Christ.

Preparation: Cut the "Heart Monitor" handout into strips on the dotted lines. Write on the plastic bag, "Words as Windows Heart Monitor." Put the strips into the bag. Set two chairs near each other. String a piece of tape across the chairs, and hang the plastic bag from it. This will serve as a heart monitor machine that the children can pass by at heart level. Choose an older child as Ivan, and you can be the doctor in the script. Give "Ivan" a copy of the "Words as Windows" script. Set up chairs on one side of the heart monitor for the class.

Items to Pack: large plastic food storage bag, masking tape, permanent marker, 2 copies of the "Words as Windows" script (p. 45), 1 copy of the "Heart Monitor" handout (p. 46)

Say: **We're going to pretend that we are Mrs. Carter's class and we're going to the hospital for a field trip. Some of you will need to undergo open-heart surgery! On the bus ride to the hospital, the talk was about the third commandment, "Speak God's name with respect." Now as you get off the bus, a heart monitor will check you. This machine will test the condition of your hearts by what you have to say.** Have the children walk, one

TOUR GUIDE TIP If you have a large class, pair the children up to read the slips of paper from the heart monitor.

at a time, by the heart monitor you have set up and take out one of the slips of paper. They should read what is on their slips of paper. Be sure that Ivan receives the slip of paper that has his name on it. If you have nonreaders in your group, pair them with readers.

Say: **The next stop on the tour of the hospital is with a surgeon who will talk to all of you.** Have the child you chose as Ivan come up, and you read the role of the doctor.

Have the kids form pairs and answer the following questions:
• **Why did some kids speak God's name without respect?**
• **Do you think Ivan's speech will change? Why or Why not?**
• **Have you ever asked God to change your heart? Would you like to?**

Say: ◗ **Our words tell what's in our hearts. A mouth that doesn't respect God shows us a heart that doesn't respect God either. As Ivan learns about God, his new heart will be filled with love and respect for God and so will his words. It may take time to learn new habits, but now he'll want to!**

Items to Pack: chalk and chalkboard

ADVENTURE IN LIVING GOD'S LAWS (10 minutes)
New Heart, New Habits

In this activity, the kids will come up with their own expressive words that don't violate God's law.

Gather the kids and say: ◗ **Our words tell what's in our hearts. As Christians, we want the whole world to know that we love and honor God. People won't believe that we honor God if they hear us use God's name without respect. Sometimes using God's name in an ugly way becomes a bad habit. Let's start a new habit.**

Have the kids brainstorm words to say when they are frustrated or surprised, such as "bummer," "rats," "goodness," and "wow." Ask them to avoid words that sound too similar to "God" or "Jesus." List their words on the chalkboard. These words are meant to replace words that take God's name in vain.

Have children form pairs and discuss the following questions with their partners.
• **What is your new-habit word?**
• **How can you remember to use a new word?**

Say: **When we become Christians, God gives us new hearts. Sometimes it takes work to create new habits. God asks us to speak his name with respect to show the whole world that we respect and honor God!**

(10 minutes)
Chameleon Christians

This simple craft game shows children how people sometimes change to suit the world.

Items to Pack: 1 plastic sandwich bag for each child, permanent markers to share

Have the children use markers to draw chameleons on their plastic bags. Have them move their chameleons from place to place so that different colors and patterns show through the plastic and the outline of the chameleon.

TOUR GUIDE TIP

You may want to copy the picture of the chameleon and place it inside the plastic bag. Then let the kids trace over the lines and remove the pattern.

SCENIC ROUTE →

Have each child cut a piece of paper to fit in the bag. Children can copy the following poem or write a prayer on the paper and place it in the bag. The paper prevents the lizard from changing colors as it is placed in different areas, just as God's word prevents sin.

Near or far,
Wherever we are,
It's always correct
To speak God's name with
respect.

Ask:

• **What happens to this chameleon as it moves from place to place?**

Say: **Some Christians are like chameleons. They change when they are with certain groups of people. When they are with their parents and at church, they speak God's name with respect. When they are with some of their friends, they misuse God's name because their friends misuse his name. Don't be a chameleon Christian! People are watching your  words to know what is in your heart!**

SOUVENIRS → (15 minutes)
How's Your Heart?

Use this craft activity to show the children the difference a pure heart can make.

Preparation: Photocopy the "How's Your Heart?" handout (page 47) onto card stock for each child. Before class, make a sample heart.

Let an older child find and read Matthew 12:34b-35. Say: **Let's make a heart that's evil and a heart that's good.**

Have the kids smudge purple crayon all over the angry heart to show that it is an evil heart. Then have the kids cut out the hearts. Cut two lengths of yarn each at least one foot long, and tape them behind the hearts. Have the kids cut apart the words, "I will speak God's name with respect" and tape them in order on the yarn behind the good heart. Then have kids cut apart the words, "I speak God's name any way I want to!" and tape them in order on the yarn behind the evil heart. The words can be pulled in and out of the mouths.

Ask:

• **What kinds of words come from a clean heart?**

• **What do we need to do to have clean hearts?**

Items to Pack: for each child, 1 copy of the "How's Your Heart?" handout (p. 47), sheet of pink card stock, pens, scissors, tape, purple crayon, yarn

SCENIC ROUTE →

It's worthwhile to invest time and money in a really nice craft project. The children feel proud of their work and might save the project for years. A few extra minutes and dollars will make the difference between trash and treasure. To make their craft a treasure, substitute thin craft foam for the paper and use the hearts as templates. The kids can write the verse from Matthew 12:34b-35 on either side of the hearts. Staple the two hearts together at the top for a "hearty" keepsake.

Items to Pack: for each child, 2 pieces of blank paper, crayon

TOUR GUIDE TIP

To respect children of all nationalities and races, avoid using brown or black as a symbol of sin. Purple is a good neutral color and will get the point across just as clearly. In the same spirit, white need not symbolize purity; gold would be a better choice.

Say: ◐ Our words tell what's in our hearts. We need to ask God to clean our hearts so that we can speak his name with respect. We want the world to know that we are God's special people, his treasure. Let's let only good words come out of our mouths.

TRAVEL-ALONG COMMANDMENT SONG (5 minutes)

Teach your kids the following four lines and the accompanying motions. Review all the verses they've learned up to this point. See pages 6-8 for the full song.

Our words tell the world what's in our hearts. *(Hold up one finger.)*
If you wanna be cool, if you wanna be smart *(hold up two fingers)*,
Speak God's name with love and respect. *(Hold up three fingers.)*
Three fingers keep your words correct. *(Cover mouth with three fingers, then take them away.)*

ONE WAY → (10 minutes)
Scribbles as Sin

This easy activity shows how scribbles on paper are like sin.

Say: As I tell this short story, scribble all over one sheet of your paper to show what happens.

Monique had a very bad habit that she had learned from her older cousin: speaking God's name without respect. She let God's name fly out of her mouth when she was mad or surprised or when she wanted to shock her little brother. Monique's words showed that she didn't have a heart that cared much about God.

Now on the other paper, draw one little line for a boy named Jeremy. Jeremy tried his whole life to please God. He never used God's name without respect—except for one time when a football hit him in the face and it hurt.

Hold up a paper filled with scribbles and one with one mark. Ask:
• What do you think will happen to Monique when she faces God?
• What do you think will happen to Jeremy?

Read James 2:10 and say: In God's eyes, sin is sin. If you've broken one commandment one time or all of them all the time, you are a sinner. God will not live with sin—neither a lot of sin nor a little sin. God knows that we can't keep his commandments and that we all sin. That's why he sent his Son, Jesus, to die for our sins. When we turn to Christ (flip over both pieces of paper), he takes all of our sins away! That's the kind of God we have, loving and forgiving. I respect God, so I'll speak his name with respect!

(5 minutes)

Before you pray, have the kids take turns addressing God respectfully in different ways, such as "Lord Almighty," "God our Father," and "Powerful Lord."

Say: **Dear God in heaven, you are good and great and mighty. You deserve all of our respect. Please help us to never misuse your name, and forgive us when we do. Help us to remember that our words tell who we are. We** want the world to know that we are followers of Jesus Christ. Help clean words come from our clean hearts. Amen.

SCENIC ROUTE →

Ask the older kids to write out the words of James 2:10 on the paper that has one little mark. Then have them each turn to a friend and explain the verse. Teach them to practice with one another and to use this as a tool to share the gospel. Ask them to turn to Romans 10:4-13 and decide which verse shows that the words coming from our mouths can be windows to our souls.

(20 minutes)

Papyrus Paper

Items to Pack: paper towels and a cookie sheet for each child, roll of white toilet paper and a cup of water for every 2 children

Who would have thought of plucking a reed growing along the Nile River, slicing it open, taking its insides out, pounding them flat, and then crisscrossing these strips and pounding them to make paper? The Egyptians did! Make your own papyrus to record God's third commandment. Plan ahead because this project will take two days to complete. Enlist extra helpers for younger kids.

1. On a cookie sheet, place lengths of toilet paper vertically so that they are touching each other. Lay more strips of toilet paper over them horizontally. Let the toilet paper flow over the edges of the cookie sheet. Weave the paper lengths so that each horizontal strip goes over and under vertical strips.

2. Continue in this manner until you have at least six layers. Be sure each layer is smooth. (If younger children can't weave the paper, don't worry about it—this is a very forgiving craft.)

3. Pour enough water over the paper to soak it thoroughly.

4. Pour off the excess water. Press down on the paper with paper towels to remove extra water. Do this several times until the paper is slightly damp. Be sure to press straight down and to keep the paper flat.

5. Let the project dry overnight.

6. When the paper is dry, carefully tear the edges away, leaving an 8x10-inch finished sheet. You can use scissors, but the torn edges look more realistic. Later, you can have the kids dampen the edges again to seal them.

7. Use a permanent marker to write the third commandment. Space the words carefully and write slowly, giving the ink time to spread into the fibers.

Extra Cool

You can make this project look more realistic by adding food coloring to the water. Papyrus is actually white, but it appears brownish because of its age. You can "age" it instantly by dissolving coffee crystals in the water or by using yellow and green food coloring. You can also make more papyrus and roll it onto two sticks to form a scroll.

Extra Cool

The Egyptians didn't use letters as we do to form each word; they used picture writing called hieroglyphics. The pictures usually went from the top of a page to the bottom. Can you write the third commandment that way? Can you think of any simple pictures to describe words? For example, the word "water" was drawn with several wavy lines. What picture could you possibly use for "speak"? Decorate your commandment page with some hieroglyphs.

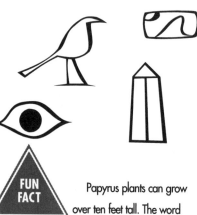

FUN FACT
Papyrus plants can grow over ten feet tall. The word "paper" comes from the word "papyrus." The name of the inner fiber of the plant, "bublio," is the source for the word "Bible." The Egyptians didn't believe in the God of the Bible. Why do you suppose the Bible earned its name from the papyrus plant?

Words as Windows

Doctor: Some of you need open-heart surgery. Your words show what's in your hearts. And for some of you there wasn't love or respect for God. We'll start with you, Ivan.

Ivan: I'm hopeless. I wish I could control my mouth!

Doctor: It's not so much a mouth problem as it is a heart problem.

Ivan: What do you mean?

Doctor: Jesus said that whatever is in your heart will come out of your mouth (Matthew 12:34b). Maybe you need a new heart.

Ivan: You can say that again.

Doctor: Maybe you need a new heart.

Ivan: Really, how do I get a new heart? I don't think anyone is going to lie down and die to give me a heart.

Doctor: Someone already did.

Ivan: No way! Who?

Doctor: Jesus did. God came to earth as a man named Jesus. Jesus did amazing miracles to show he was God and then died on the cross to take away all of our sins. He wants to give you a new heart to follow him.

Ivan: I need a new heart. How do I do that?

Doctor: You simply pray, asking God to forgive you. Believe that Jesus paid for your sins on the cross. Trust him. Let him be your Lord.

Ivan: I'm ready to do that.

Doctor: Congratulations! The Bible says you have been given a new heart—one that wants to follow, obey, and love God. With your new heart, you'll learn new words to speak God's name with respect. Is anyone else ready for open-heart surgery?

Heart Monitor

• Jordan said, "I try to speak God's name with respect."

• Emily laughed, "Ha! Ha! What is that—a joke? Speak God's name with respect? No one speaks my name with respect."

• Natasha said, "I will speak God's name with respect. I love God and honor him, but once in a while, a bad word slips out."

• Nathan said, "I try to speak God's name with respect. I don't say his name, unless I am praying directly to him."

• Ivan said, "Speak God's name with respect? What's the big deal? Everyone talks like that!"

• Christopher said, "My big brother doesn't speak God's name with respect. He always cusses. And he's cool."

• Reba remarked, "Even on TV, no one speaks God's name with respect. So who cares if I do?"

• Shayn said, "I know that I should speak God's name with respect. But I usually don't. It's just a bad habit for me. I can quit anytime I want to."

• Brianna bragged, "Come on. God doesn't care what I say. Why does he get all upset if people don't speak his name with respect?"

• Alec said, "I don't really understand what that means, 'Speak God's name with respect.' What does that have to do with swear words? What a useless rule!"

How's Your Heart?

"I speak God's name any way I want!"

"I will speak God's name with respect."

JOURNEY 5

The Fourth Commandment: Set Aside a Special Day for God

Pathway Point: 🌐 God gives us a day to refuel and remember him.

TOUR GUIDE TIP

Enlarge the fourth commandment on page 10, and make a copy for each child in your class. Have crayons or markers available so children arriving early or leaving late can color and decorate the pages for their notebooks.

TOUR GUIDE TIP

The activities in this book were designed for multi-age groups. Select from the activities or adapt them as needed for your class.

TOUR GUIDE TIP

Most Christians observe Sunday as the Sabbath. However, some families celebrate the Sabbath on a Saturday. Tell the children that which day they set aside as a special day is not important. What counts is that we take time out from our busy schedules to reflect and recharge.

Items to Pack: flashlight; six clear, plastic, disposable cups

In-Focus Verse: "Remember the Sabbath day by keeping it holy. Six days you shall labor and do all your work, but the seventh day is a Sabbath to the Lord your God. On it you shall not do any work, neither you, nor your son or daughter, nor your manservant or maidservant, nor your animals, nor the alien within your gates. For in six days the Lord made the heavens and the earth, the sea, and all that is in them, but he rested on the seventh day. Therefore the Lord blessed the Sabbath day and made it holy" (Exodus 20:8-11).

Travel Itinerary

In our competitive, achievement-oriented society, kids, as well as adults, dash at breakneck speed from one task to the next. Before we know what has happened, we're burned out. We snap at each other, become physically exhausted, and feel alienated from God. If this describes you, you've probably been ignoring God's fourth commandment: Set aside a special day for God.

Our busy world bombards us with responsibilities. Our spheres of work and school accost us with draining duties and, sometimes, ungodly values and profane speech. Even kids can have exhausting schedules full of sports, lessons, parties, church activities, and homework. How we need a special day to re-energize our bodies and rekindle our spirits! God, in his kindness, commands us to jump off our dizzying merry-go-rounds into his arms. He recognizes our needs even when we refuse to. He's waiting to renew our strength. Remember the Sabbath, and teach your children to do the same.

DEPARTURE PRAYER (5 minutes)

Corporate worship involves corporate prayer. Whenever possible, include all the children in prayer time. Consider photocopying a prayer for the kids to read aloud with you. Have the younger kids draw a prayer to God while you read yours.

Say: **Dear God, you are so smart to think of such a wonderful plan. Thank you for giving us one free day. Thank you for giving us this special time to refuel and reflect on you and your goodness. Thank you for making us your people—set apart as special. Help us to keep your commandments. Amen.**

1st STOP DISCOVERY (10 minutes)
Starting Bright, Losing Light

In this activity, cups serve as filters over a flashlight to show how we can lose our light.

Darken the room. Say: **We live in a dark world that often forgets God. We come together at church** (turn on the flashlight) **to remember God and fill up on his love! When we are around other Christians, we glow like this light. It's as though our batteries are recharged.**

Have six children each add a plastic cup to the lens of the flashlight. As they add the cups, ask them to name something they do on each particular day of the week. For example, a child might say, "On Tuesdays I go to school and ice-skating practice."

When all six cups have been added, ask:

• **What do you notice about the light?**

• **How is this like the way our weeks go?**

• **What can we do to get our lights to shine brightly again?**

Take away the cups so the light shines brightly. Say: **This flashlight shines brightly because its batteries are fully charged. As the cups were added, the light got dimmer, as though the batteries were running out of power. That's how it is for us as Christians. When we worship, we get our batteries charged so we can zoom through a busy week.** 🌑 God knew we needed a special day to refuel and remember him, so he gave us his fourth law: Set aside a special day for God.

SCENIC ROUTE → Write the commandment on poster board before class, and hang it on a wall. For extra impact, shine the light on the commandment as the children read it with you.

STORY EXCURSION (15 minutes)
LaKeisha Refuels and Remembers God

In this activity, children will move from station to station, drinking juice to see how their fuel is depleted.

Preparation: Write a different day of the week on each piece of paper, and create Monday through Saturday stations by taping the papers to the wall or to chairs placed around the room. Arrange other chairs in a circle away from the stations. These chairs will represent church on Sunday. Read the story about LaKeisha, and decide what props and actions you may want to add.

Items to Pack: disposable cup for each child, permanent markers, juice, newspaper, 7 pieces of blank paper, masking tape

Have the kids make "Fill 'Er Up" cups, marking them as shown in the following illustration. Choose an older child to be LaKeisha. Begin by having everyone sit in "church."

Say: **LaKeisha loved going to church. She had lots of friends there. They sang songs, read Bible stories, and talked about important things. LaKeisha learned about God and loved him. It was like having her gas tank filled up.** (*Lead the kids in a praise song. Fill their cups to the top with juice. Tell them to sip until the juice has reached the line marked Monday.*) **LaKeisha was ready to zoom through the week ahead.** (*Have the kids follow "LaKeisha" to the Monday station, taking care to not spill their juice.*)

On Monday, LaKeisha went off to school in a great mood. Then she heard Sarah whispering to Emily, "LaKeisha wore the weirdest shoes today!"

Emily laughed back, "I wouldn't be caught dead in those shoes!"

LaKeisha's shoulders drooped. She felt as though she had been in a car crash. Ugh. (*Have all the kids sip their juice down to the Tuesday mark and follow LaKeisha to the Tuesday station.*)

On Tuesday, LaKeisha missed half of the words on her spelling test. And she had really studied. With a big sigh, LaKeisha picked up her backpack and lugged home

SCENIC ROUTE → To add visual impact to this activity, create a "road" by placing masking tape along the floor or using a wipe-off crayon (if your floor is linoleum). Begin the road at Sunday, and design it to meander around the room, going off course as it gets farther from Sunday.

four big textbooks to study that night. No time to read her Bible. LaKeisha felt as though she had taken a wrong turn and was lost. *(Have the kids go off course, face the wall, and sip to the Wednesday mark.)*

On Wednesday night, LaKeisha got sick. She didn't even make it to the bathroom before she threw up. *(Have the kids move to the Thursday station and sip to the level marked Thursday.)*

On Thursday, LaKeisha felt well enough to go to school. But she had so much homework that she was late to her softball game. When LaKeisha ran onto the field, she realized she had her shirt on backward. LaKeisha said to Lisa, "I wish I could throw myself into reverse!"

"What are you talking about?" Lisa asked.

"Never mind," LaKeisha said as she missed a grounder. *(Have kids move to the Friday station and sip their juice to the Friday mark.)*

"I'm glad it's Friday," LaKeisha thought to herself. But it was a rough afternoon. At recess, the kids were using swear words. When LaKeisha wouldn't swear, Jeremy Jackson called her "Little Miss Goody Two Shoes." She came close to slugging him. LaKeisha felt as though she had been bombarded by the world. *(Have the kids wad up sheets of newspaper and throw them at LaKeisha. Then have kids sip their juice to the level marked Saturday and move to the Saturday station.)*

I'll get a break on Saturday, LaKeisha thought. No chance. Her mom handed her a broom. All morning she and her mom cleaned the garage. In the afternoon, she got in a fight with her little sister. After softball practice, LaKeisha fell into bed exhausted. "I am completely out of gas," she said. *(Have the kids finish their drinks and move to the Sunday station.)*

On Sunday morning, the last thing LaKeisha wanted to do was drag herself out of bed and go to church. But she remembered the fourth commandment: "Set aside a special day for God." So she walked to the neighbors' house and climbed in their car with them. She wondered how they could be so wide-awake when she was still trying to finish her dream. But at church, her Sunday school teacher hugged her. *(Have kids hug each other.)* Her friends congratulated her on her home run Thursday night. *(Have kids high-five each other.)* They read what Jesus said in the Bible *(have a child read Mark 2:27)*: "The Sabbath was made for man, not man for the Sabbath."

When the teacher asked the class what that could mean, LaKeisha's hand shot up. "It means that 🌙 God gives us a special day to refuel and remember him. He asks us to set aside one day a week and spend it with him."

"Exactly," the teacher said. "The Sabbath is like a present from God."

"Cool," three kids said together.

LaKeisha zoomed into children's church. She gulped down every word of the message. Even the songs seemed to rev up her engine. *(Have the kids sing a favorite praise song.)*

After church, her family went to the lake for a picnic. LaKeisha sat on the end of the dock, just watching the clouds change shapes. She thought, "What an awesome God. He actually commands us to have fun! I'm so glad I set aside a special day for this really cool, wonderful God." *(Fill the cups of those kids who want another drink.)*

SCENIC ROUTE → You can extend this activity for the older kids. Have them rinse out their "Fill 'Er Up" cups. On the top rim, they can write "re" with permanent marker. Then have them cut one-third off the top of another cup and place the first cup inside it. Have them look up words in a dictionary that start with "re" and describe things to do on a Sabbath day, such as "rejoice," "renew," "refocus," "refresh," "recharge," "relax," "rest," and "remember." On the shorter cup they can write the letters that come after "re" for the words they chose. As they turn the bottom cup, the letters they wrote will line up with the "re" to make words.

Have the kids form pairs to discuss the following questions:

• **Why did LaKeisha lose energy during the week?**

• **How do you lose energy and enthusiasm for God during your week?**

• **What can you do about it?**

Say: God commanded us to set aside a special day for him. In his kindness,  God gives us a day to refuel and remember him. Then he asks us to give it back to him as we rejoice at church and relax afterward. God knows what we need and gives it to us. Isn't he wonderful?

ADVENTURE IN LIVING GOD'S LAWS

(15 minutes) Work, Work, Worship

In this activity kids will rotate from one exercise station to the next and relax on Sunday.

Preparation: Retain the Monday through Saturday stations and church setup from the story about LaKeisha. If possible, set up Sunday on carpeting. Write each of the following exercises on a piece of paper: sit-ups, jumping jacks, deep knee bends, push-ups, running in place, and leg lifts. For nonreaders, draw stick figures. (You may use any exercises you choose; these are only examples.) Post an exercise sign at each of the Monday through Saturday stations.

Tell the kids that God planned for us to work six days and then to rest and remember him on the seventh. Have the kids rotate by groups from one station to the next, doing the exercises posted at each station.

When all the kids have been to all the stations, ask:

• **What did you do Monday through Saturday?**

• **How is this like your week?**

• **Why did God command us to set aside a special day for him?**

Say: God knows us. He knows that we will run around until we wear ourselves out and forget all about him. That's why God thinks it's so important to set aside a special day for him. Really, it's for us. God is so thoughtful to give us a day to refuel and remember him. Have the kids gather in the Sunday station, and reward them with a special treat. You may want to supply pillows or beanbags for them to rest on. Have them take turns reading related passages from the Bible, such as Leviticus 23:3; Hebrews 10:23-25; and Psalm 100.

(15 minutes) Commandment Commercial

Have the older kids work in teams to make up commercials to convince the public to set aside a special day for God. Have the younger kids provide the TV show that is being interrupted. For example, younger children can be in Bobo's circus, juggling, singing, or showing off other talents. Then the younger ones will watch the commercials the older kids have created.

When the commercials are over, let the older kids ask the younger ones the following questions.

• **What did our commercial try to get you to do?**

• **What are some things that refresh you?**

• **Why is this so important to God?**

Items to Pack: paper, whistle, treats

SCENIC ROUTE →

Make this game more realistic by adding real work to the stations. For example, you could require kids to answer math problems, peel potatoes, read flashcards, fold towels, practice penmanship, and use a dictionary to define a list of words.

SCENIC ROUTE →

Celebrate Sunday with sundaes! Supply ice cream, cherries, whipped cream, and toppings to make Super Sunday Sundaes.

SOUVENIRS (20 minutes)

Refuel With Raisins

In this activity, children will get new fuel on Sunday for the fuel they use throughout the week.

Give everyone a "Refueled With Raisins" handout and all the materials needed to complete this craft. For each day of the week, have the children color in the "fuel gauge." Then have everyone cut out the completed circle and glue it onto a plate. Have kids write the fourth commandment in their own words under the fuel gauge. Then have them cut out the arrow and attach it to the middle of the gauge with a brass fastener.

Have older kids write in each weekday's space the activities that fill that day. Have younger kids draw pictures. When the craft is complete, give each child six raisins to put on the Sunday slot. Say: **We all work hard during the week at school and at home, so God gave us one special day called the Sabbath. He wants us to use that day to be re-filled with energy and his love.**

Have the kids form pairs. The partners will take turns telling each other what they do on each day of the week. As they discuss each day, they will eat one raisin and move the arrow and their remaining raisins to the next day. By Saturday, their "tanks" will register empty. Have partners discuss the following questions:

- **What happened after a whole week went by?**
- **How is this like your life?**
- **What can you do on Sunday to get filled up again?**

Say: God made us like a car that runs out of gas every six days. ◐ **He gives us a special day to refuel and remember him since we are his people. God even showed us how, when he made the world in six days and rested on the seventh day. Ask your parents to take you to church. If they can't, ask a friend to take you. Many churches have buses that will pick you up. Remember God!**

Have the kids cut out the commandment bracelets from the handouts, fold them, put them around their wrists, and tape the ends together. When they get home, they can share the bracelets with their parents.

TOUR GUIDE TIP

When working on a craft with a large group of children, it is much easier if the group works on the same step at the same time. Since the older children will complete each stage before the younger children, assign each of them to help a younger child. Wait until the entire group has finished each stage, then move together to the next stage.

TRAVEL-ALONG COMMANDMENT SONG (5 minutes)

Teach the children the following stanza and accompanying motions, and then add it to what they've already learned. See pages 6-8 for the full song.

Hold up four fingers, and push them away *(hold up four fingers, and push away.)*

To set aside a special day. *(Slowly move your hand across your chest.)*

Refuel your engines and remember God. *(Wave four fingers on one hand, then the other.)*

Get to a church where he's worshipped and awed. *(Raise hands up.)*

(10 minutes)
And in This Corner...

This activity illustrates that it is belief, not obedience, that makes us acceptable to God.

Items to Pack: string or streamers, tape, index cards

Set up a boxing ring by attaching the string around four chairs. Have the kids set up chairs on opposite sides of the ring.

Ask:

• **Who is really acceptable to God—the one who *obeys* God's commandments or the one who *believes* in Jesus Christ?**

The kids will choose one of two sides to sit on. Team A thinks that *believing* in Jesus is the way to be acceptable to God. Team B thinks that *obeying* God's commandments is the way. Let each team choose someone to be a "fighter" for his or her team. On Team A's card, write "belief" and tape it to the fighter. On Team B's card, write "obey" and tape it to the boxer. Put the two boxers in the ring.

Say: **Many people in the world are confused about the question, "What is the way to be acceptable to God, to believe or obey?"** Pause as you say "believe" and "obey." Have Team A stand up and cheer when you say "believe." Ask the fighter to box the air. Do the same for Team B when you say "obey."

Say: **Most people believe that if they obey most of the commandments, they'll be acceptable to God. Listen carefully while I read you these two verses and then tell me what they say in your own words. "This is love for God: to obey his commands"** (1 John 5:3a). **"Yet to all who received him, to those who believed in his name, he gave the right to become children of God"** (John 1:12). Have the children tell you what the verses say in their own words.

First you believe in Jesus, and then you show your love for him by obeying God's commandments. If you believe in Jesus, you are acceptable to God, even though you'll sometimes mess up and break a commandment. Let's say John 1:12 together. "Yet to all who received him, to those who believed in his name, he gave the right to become children of God."

First John 5:3b says, "His commands are not burdensome." Talk about how we often don't feel like going to church but we always feel glad after we have. Have the kids write the fourth commandment on a piece of paper and then help one another tape the papers to their backs. Then have them try to remember, write on each other's papers, and carry the other commandments. How heavy are his commandments?

(5 minutes)

Have the kids stand along the walls all around the room. As you start praying, have them come together, hold hands, and silently form a circle.

Say: **Dear Lord our God, we come to you from our busy world. We come together with our Christian brothers and sisters to praise you and remember how awesome you are. Thank you for loving us enough to order us to set aside a special day for you. Help us to set aside time every day to think about you. We love you. Amen.**

Next week's commandment, "Honor your father and mother," offers opportunities for the kids to do just that. Have your kids make invitations to their parents to stay an extra fifteen minutes after class. You may want to bring in some doughnuts or ask the kids to bring in something to help honor their parents, such as flowers or drawings.

BACK ROAD TO WRITING

(10 minutes)

When in Rome, Write As the Romans Do

In Roman times, papyrus was used for important papers. Since it was expensive, the children wrote in writing tablets called diptychs. These tablets were made in a wooden frame. Melted wax was poured into the center of the frame. When the wax was hard, the children etched their words on it with a pointed stick. To use the tablet again, the wax was softened with a candle flame and smoothed. Make your own wax diptych.

1. Have each child glue the craft sticks onto the center of the paper to form a square.

2. Melt the candy bark in the microwave, several squares at a time, and stir. (Follow the directions on the package.) This "wax" gets very hot very quickly, so let it cool before allowing the kids to work with it. Use a spoon to scoop some candy bark into each frame.

3. Smooth out the candy bark. Before it hardens (but after it has congealed), show children how to use the pencil to write out the commandment. Make sure you can see the black paper beneath it. Shorten the commandment to "Set aside a day for God." Let the younger ones just write "God."

4. Let the candy harden for five to ten minutes. You may speed up the process by putting it in the refrigerator.

5. Have children store their crafts in resealable plastic bags.

Extra Cool

We use Latin words in our language today. You can add a real Latin word to your commandment. The initials N.B. stand for "nota bene," which means "note well." It reminds us of Jesus' words: "He who has ears to hear." You can add N.B. to your commandment to note well to remember the Sabbath day. Which Roman numeral would you use for the fourth commandment?

Did You Know?

Did you know that about half of all English words today originated in or came from Latin, the language of the Roman Empire? Although Latin is not spoken today, it is still an important school subject. Until the 1900s, men and women in college had to read and write Latin.

Items to Pack: heavy glass bowl, microwave, and, for each child, 4 wide craft sticks, glue stick, heavy black paper, pencil, square of white candy bark, resealable plastic bag, spoon

FUN FACT

Some of these writing tablets were made out of black wax. The marks were etched into the black all the way to the white wood below. You can use chocolate bark and smooth it out over white paper if you want to make your tablet even more realistic. It's the contrast that makes the words stand out. Which do you prefer for correcting mistakes: reheating wax or using the eraser on the end of your pencil?

Refuel With Raisins

Monday Tuesday Wednesday Thursday Friday Saturday SUNDAY!

E   F

Commandment Bracelet

Mom and Dad, please take me to church.

We can set aside a special day for God.

The Fifth Commandment:
Honor Your Father and Mother

Pathway Point: 🌐 Honor means respect and obey.

In-Focus Verse: "Honor your father and your mother, so that you may live long in the land the Lord your God is giving you" (Exodus 20:12).

Travel Itinerary

Gone are the days of father knows best. Now we have Lisa Simpson reprimanding her weird dad, Homer. Gone are the days of Arthur Maxwell's stories about loving direction from a wise parent. Many children in your classroom come from single-parent, blended, or other nontraditional two-parent families. Kids today are bombarded with books, media, and friends denigrating the role of parents. The word and concept of "honor" are completely foreign to many children today.

Even parents are confused as to what's best for their children's psychological well-being. They ask, for example, if kids should express their anger or learn to hold their tongues. As always, God's ways are the healthiest—mentally, physically, and spiritually. Polite, respectful children are not a byproduct of chance. Basically, kids must be taught everything. As Christian educators, we teach children God's way: Honor your father and mother. Our job is akin to pushing snow back up a mountain in the wake of an avalanche. Let this chapter help you guide children along God's path.

DEPARTURE PRAYER (5 minutes)

Jesus addressed God in an intriguing way. He acknowledged that God is our Father whose lap we sit upon. That same God is the ruler of the universe! Talk to the kids about God as the almighty ruler and the loving Father. As you pray the following prayer, invite the kids to join you in kneeling before him and then sitting on their chairs, as though they were climbing onto their daddy's laps, because God is our Daddy.

Say: **Our Father in heaven, you are holy. Your commandments are wise. You ask us to honor our fathers and mothers. Please help us to understand what that means. Help us to obey you by respecting and obeying our parents. Sometimes it feels as though the world around us would rather forget you and your commandments. But not us, Lord. Help us to honor our parents and, in so doing, honor you. Amen.**

1st STOP DISCOVERY (10 minutes)
Worth Their Weight

In this activity, children will race to a scale to honor their parents.

TOUR GUIDE TIP
Enlarge the fifth commandment on page 10, and make a copy for each child in your class. Have crayons or markers available so children arriving early or leaving late can color and decorate the pages for their notebooks.

TOUR GUIDE TIP
The activities in this book have been designed for multi-age groups. Select from the activities or adapt them as needed for your class.

SCENIC ROUTE →
Consider inviting the parents of your students to a reception in their honor after class. Serve a snack, let the parents read the Declaration of Dependence, and have the kids show their Souvenirs. Have the kids sing the new stanza of the "Travel-Along Commandment Song." Have kids reenact the prayer archway, and let them tell something about their parents that honors them.

Items to Pack: 2 scales (either from home or homemade), bag of pennies

Use this relay race to show kids the importance of their parents. Set up the scale on one end of the room, and keep the pennies on the other side. Form the children into two teams, making sure to balance the age levels in each group.

Say: **When God told us to honor our fathers and mothers, he used a funny word for honor—"kabed." The word means giving our parents a lot of pounds or weight.** 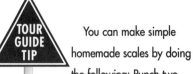 **Honoring your father and mother means respecting and obeying them because they are very important people. In fact, they're worth their weight in gold!**

Give the kids five minutes to complete this activity. Have them take turns taking a penny from the bag and going to the scales. As each child drops a penny on the scale, he or she must state a reason his or her parents are important. For example, one child might add a penny and say, "I honor my parents because they teach me right from wrong." That child would then return to his or her team and tag the next child, who would repeat the process. After five minutes, ask:

- **How is saying good things about your parents honoring them?**
- **What are some ways you can show them honor today?**

Say: **You can obey God's commandment to** 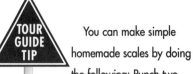 **honor your mother and father by respecting and obeying them today!**

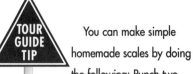

TOUR GUIDE TIP

You can make simple homemade scales by doing the following: Punch two holes near the rims in each of two paper cups or paper bowls. Feed a chenille wire across and through the holes on each cup to form handles. Loop rubber bands through the chenille wires for the baskets to dangle from. Hang these from the ends of a dowel or other stick, and hang the stick by a string.

Also, during this activity, be certain that the younger children know they should never put coins in their mouths.

STORY EXCURSION (15 minutes)
Jacquie Learns the Hard Way

From this story, the children will learn about respecting and obeying their parents.

Items to Pack: piece of paper with a simple drawing of a thumb pointing down

Tell the children that you are going to tell a story about a girl named Jacquie. Tell them that each time Jacquie or another child dishonors a parent, you will hold up the thumbs-down card and the kids will say "boo!" When you put the picture away, the kids will stop booing. As you tell the story, pause to see if the kids respond before you give them the thumbs-down signal.

Say: **Jacquie's mom was talking on the phone. Jacquie tugged on her mom's shirt and said, "Mom, can I go with Brittany to see a movie?"**

Her mother held up a finger to say, "Just a minute."

"Hurry up," Jacquie scolded her mom. "You're always gabbing." (Boo!)

"What movie is it?" Jacquie's mom asked, hanging up the phone.

"Uh, something like *Night Light on Main Street*," Jacquie said.

"What's its rating?"

"How am I supposed to know?" (Boo!)

Jacquie's mom opened the newspaper to the movie section. "*Night Fright on Main Street*? It's PG-13. Of course you can't go."

Jacquie moaned, "But Mom, everybody's seen it. You're mean!" (Boo!)

"You know that I won't let you see a PG-13 movie because I love you too much to let you hurt your mind."

When Jacquie's mom turned around, Jacquie mocked her mom, mumbling, "You know that I won't let you see a PG-13 movie!" (Boo!) **Her mother spun around.**

Jacquie just rolled her eyes and stomped off (Boo!) to call Brittany, muttering, "All my friends get to do what they want!" (Boo!)

When Jacquie picked up the phone, she got an idea. Glancing at her mom, she pretended to dial Brittany's home. She spoke to the dial tone. "I'm sorry, Brittany, I can't go...What?...Sounds good...Let me ask my mom." (Boo!)

Jacquie covered the phone and yelled, "Mom, is it OK if I go with their family and we just hang out at the mall?"

"Sure, honey."

Jacquie hung up. Without looking at her mom's face, she went outside to wait for Brittany. She hoped her mother didn't see that she wasn't wearing the hat that her mother always insisted on. (Boo!) When Brittany's family arrived, Jacquie hopped in their car, and they zoomed off to the movie.

While they were standing in line, Jacquie said to Brittany, "I'm lucky to be here. You know, I had to pretend I called you. My stupid mom doesn't let me see PG-13 movies." (Boo!)

"Why not?" Brittany asked.

"Because she's so weird. (Boo!) If she had her way, I'd spend my entire life locked in my bedroom, reading educational books!"

"Moms and dads can be a such a pain," Brittany replied. (Boo!)

Even though Jacquie tried to close her eyes during the scary parts of *Night Fright*, she still heard the screams. It seemed as though the crazy murderer would leap off the screen at her. "I wish I had never come," she thought. "This movie is disgusting."

That night Jacquie wanted to sleep with the light on, but her little sister kept complaining. Tossing and turning, Jacquie finally fell asleep.

At midnight the whole household was awakened by a bloodcurdling scream. Jacquie's mom raced into Jacquie's room and flicked on the lights. Jacquie was sitting up in her bed, holding her knees to her chest and shaking.

"Mom, I had the worst dream! It was just like the mov..." Jacquie stopped.

"You went to see that movie, didn't you?"

Jacquie hung her head and whispered, "Yes. I'm sorry, Mom."

"I'm sorry too," her mom replied, "I made that rule for your benefit, not mine. I'm sorry for your sake that you chose to disobey me. Go back to sleep. We'll discuss this in the morning."

Ask:

• What are some ways Jacquie dishonored her mother?

• How did she break God's fifth commandment?

• When you don't feel like honoring your parents, what should you do?

Say: ◑ God told us to honor our fathers and mothers, which means obeying them and treating them with respect. It also means speaking to them and about them in nice ways. It can be really tough to do this when we're mad at them, but God doesn't just ask us to honor our parents, he *commands* it!

SCENIC ROUTE →
Go through the movie reviews in the newspaper, and ask kids how they think God would feel about certain movies. Discuss why some filmmakers would deliberately include profanity, nudity, and violence in their movies. To teach the children discernment, let them make up titles of movies that would violate certain commandments. For example, a title violating the ninth commandment, would be *Lies: Sweet and Innocent*. Have the kids suggest alternative Christian titles that honor each commandment.

(10 minutes)
Declaration of Dependence

In this activity, the children will sign your commitment to follow God's ways.

Preparation: Hang the mural paper on the wall. Write the following, making the first letter of each sentence large and fancy. Leave room for kids to write their own responses and sign their names under the words you write.

I Will Respect and Obey My Parents.

I Promise to Honor My Father and Mother by _____.

Signed by _____

Say: **When Thomas Jefferson wrote the Declaration of Independence, the colonists wanted to form a new country, set apart from Britain. When God gave Moses the Ten Commandments, God was forming a new people for himself—a people set apart from the behavior of the rest of the world. Now we Christians are God's people, and we promise to follow his ways. If you promise to obey God's commandment to honor your parents, sign this declaration.**

Have the older kids write one way to honor their parents on the mural and sign their names. Ask the younger children to tell the group what they will do and write their names if they are able. If not, write their names for them.

(20 minutes)
Sass or Pout—You're Out!

The children will learn how to honor their parents' requests.

Preparation: Photocopy the "Watching Our Responses" cards onto card stock, and cut them apart. If you have more than twenty kids, create enough sets for each group of twenty to have one set. Assign some of the older kids to help the nonreaders, and make sure that at least one child receives a star card.

Ask one child to play the parent in this game. Let each of the other children select a response card. Have kids stand and form a circle. Tell them that when the "parent" says, "It's time to feed the dog," the child to the parent's right will read his or her response aloud. If the child reads a starred response, he or she will remain standing; if not, he or she will sit down. Continue around the circle until each child has read a response. The children who remain standing are examples of how to honor parents. If there is time, play several rounds, reshuffling and letting the kids choose new cards each time.

After the last round, gather the children and ask:

• **How did some of the responses honor the parent?**

• **How would your parents feel if you responded with some of the sassy comments we just heard?**

• **The next time your parents ask you to do something you don't want to, how will you answer them?**

Have a child read Ephesians 6:1-3. Say: **The Bible says that if you honor your parents, you'll live a long life. That's one reason to obey. However, the most important**

TOUR GUIDE TIP

Reread the response card that begins, "I really don't have time because..." Say: If you were to say this to your parents, you would be honoring them, even though you would not be agreeing. You would be explaining in a respectful way why you can't feed the dog. Most parents are reasonable if you talk to them using respectful words. You can disagree with your parents, but do it with respect.

reason is that God tells us to. It's sometimes very hard to do, but when you respect and obey God by  honoring your father and mother, your life will be happier.

Watching Our Responses

SOUVENIRS (20 minutes)

This exercise will be a visual reminder to kids to keep the right responses handy.

Preparation: Make a sample to use as an example.

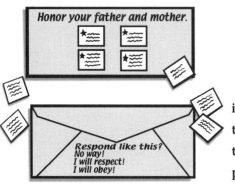
Give each child a set of the "Watching Our Responses" cards (page 63) and an envelope. Have kids cut apart the cards and put them in the envelope, leaving out the cards with the stars. Have the children write on the backs of their envelopes, "Respond like this? No way! I will respect! I will obey!" (Have the older kids help the younger ones write.) To the front of the envelope, have kids glue the four starred cards. Above the cards, have them write, "Honor your father and mother." Have them seal the envelopes to signify that they will not use the kinds of answers that are on the cards inside.

Ask:

• What are some answers to parents that you should not use?

• What are some answers that honor your parents?

• How can you use this as a reminder to honor your parents?

Say: We have all been disrespectful to our parents at one time or another. Following God's commandment to honor your parents is hard to do. There will be many times you won't want to respect and obey them. Remember that God's special people try to honor their parents. Put this envelope in your room as a reminder to honor your parents. Ask God, and he will help you honor them, even when you don't feel like it.

TRAVEL-ALONG COMMANDMENT SONG (5 minutes)

Teach the children the following stanza and accompanying motions, and then add it to what they've already learned. See pages 6-8 for the full song.

Hey, put your five fingers way down low. *(Push hand down near knees.)*
Honor your parents is the way to go. *(Slowly raise hand.)*
God gave you parents when you were small. *(Slowly raise hand.)*
Respect and obey them while you're growing tall. *(Slowly raise hand.)*

Death Row

ONE WAY (15 minutes)

In this activity, the children will break out of a jail made out of streamers symbolizing God's law.

Preparation: Cut ten streamers each about five feet long. Write a different commandment on each streamer.

Form a jail by hanging streamers from the ceiling. This will represent a jail made of God's laws. Read each of the commandments individually, pausing after each to ask the

kids if they've broken it. Children who admit to having broken the commandment must go into the jail.

Say: **Sometimes God's rules can feel like bars on a jail cell. Breaking God's laws is sin. When we break God's good and loving laws, they become like prison bars, and we become like prisoners sitting on death row. Like us, the Apostle Paul realized he was on death row as a prisoner to sin. Are we all doomed? Let's hear what he wrote in the book of Romans:** "All the world stands hushed and guilty before Almighty God...No one can ever be made right in God's sight by doing what the law commands" (Romans 3:19b-20a, *The Living Bible*).

Ask:

• **How are God's commands like prison bars?**

• **What can we do about it?**

Read: "But now God has shown us a different way to heaven...Now God says he will...declare us 'not guilty'—if we trust Jesus Christ to take away our sins. And we all can be saved in this same way, by coming to Christ, no matter who we are or what we have been like" (Romans 3:21a-22, *TLB*). **Can you believe it? We can be free!**

Ask:

• **What do you have to do to get off death row?**

• **Are you ready to come to Christ?**

Say: **You may notice that God doesn't change his commandments to get you off death row. Jesus simply paid the Judge, his Father. The price was perfection; the payment was his blood.** As children walk out of "death row" through the streamers, ask them to state their understanding of Christ's payment for their sin.

<table>
<tr><td>

HOME AGAIN PRAYER

</td><td>

(5 minutes)

For this prayer, have the kids stand and form two rows, face to face. Say: **In a military wedding, the attendants form an archway of swords as a way of honoring the bride and groom. Today we're going to form an archway to honor our parents.**

</td></tr>
</table>

Have each child touch the hands of the child facing him or her to form an archway. Starting at one end, have each child walk under the archway, thanking God for his or her parents. For example, one child might say, "Thank you, Lord, for my mom and dad. I honor them because they give me such good food to eat."

TOUR GUIDE TIP You may want to use this time as a review, seeing which commandments the children can recall as you write them. Or you may ask older children to write each commandment. The more you can involve the children, the more meaningful their class time will be.

TOUR GUIDE TIP Does knowing that Jesus Christ freed you from death row make you want to dance? Does it make you want to shout this good news from the rooftops? If not, you may need to do some soul-searching and think about starting fresh with Jesus. Never be ashamed to ask questions and to be honest with God. Reread Romans 3 and Romans 6. Ask questions. Wrestle with God and your pride until you are sure that you, too, are free from the bondage of the Law.

BACK ROAD TO WRITING

(15 minutes)

Ivory Etchings

Ivory has been treasured in many cultures, from the Romans to the Japanese to the Eskimos. Important documents and intricate pictures were etched into the bone. The Eskimos, or Inuit Indians, carved pictures into walrus tusks. Then they stained the etchings. This art form is called "scrimshaw."

1. Place a bar of soap in the glass bowl, and microwave it on high for fifty seconds or until the soap softens.

2. Place a piece of wax paper on a cookie sheet. Pour the softened soap onto the wax paper. Smooth it out, and flatten it to form a square about ¼ inch thick. (You may want to cover it with a towel if it's too hot to touch.)

3. When the soap cools and hardens, trim off the sides to form straight edges.

4. Use a pen to etch the fifth commandment into the soap. The etching doesn't need to reach the wax paper.

5. Dip a brush into the paint, and fill in the etching.

6. Carefully glue the etching on the paper.

....

Did You Know?

Did you know that there is an international ban on ivory? That means in most countries around the world it is against the law to buy or sell ivory. That's because people kill the animals—mostly elephants—just for their tusks. Too many elephants have been killed just so that someone, somewhere, could have some ivory.

....

Watching Our Responses

Say, "I'm sick of that job!"	Grumble, "So?"	Say, "Why can't somebody else do it?"	Grumble, "It's *always* time to feed the dog!"
☆ Say, "Sure, where's the dog food?"	Say, "No."	Complain, "I hate that job. That smelly food makes me sick!"	Say, "I thought I already did."
Whine, "I fed the dog yesterday. Why does that dog eat so much?"	Yell, "I don't want to!"	☆ Say, "OK, I'll do it right now."	Mutter, "I didn't hear that."
Say, "Yeah, yeah, later, later."	Whine, "Why can't Dad [or Mom] do it?"	Say, "OK, but I'm busy playing right now."	Mutter, "Why do I have to?"
Say, "OK, OK, after I finish watching TV."	☆ Say, "Yes, ma'am" or "Yes, sir."	☆ Say, "I really don't have time because I'm leaving for soccer practice. If Taryn will do it tonight, I'll do it tomorrow."	Say, "You're so mean!"

JOURNEY 7

The Sixth Commandment:
You Shall Not Kill

Pathway Point: 🌑 Say *no* to violence! Say *yes* to life!

In-Focus Verse: "You shall not murder" (Exodus 20:13).

Travel Itinerary

We feed kids a steady diet of moral poison in the comfort of their own homes and then wonder why kids kill. Murder, death, and violence assault young eyes in full, living color. Our children consume popcorn as they become passive partners to the crimes they mentally ingest. Eric Harris and Dylan Klebold watched a movie called *Natural Born Killers* repeatedly before they planned the slaughter at Columbine High School in Littleton, Colorado.

All human life is precious to God. Violent games and movies make it seem like nothing to take a life. We need to teach children to protect themselves against violence on TV and in movies, video games, and music. This lesson seeks to give the children practical tools to enable them to say *no* to violence and *yes* to respecting life.

DEPARTURE PRAYER (5 minutes)

This lesson reveals the dichotomy between the world's values and God's. Tell the kids that Christians are all on the same team, and form a prayer huddle as you say the following prayer.

Say: **Dear Lord our God, when you commanded, "Do not kill," TV hadn't even been invented, but violence had. You were so sad about the violent world that you wiped it out with a flood. Help us to realize that all of life is precious. We want to stand with you when you say, "Choose life." Help us to say *no* to violence and *yes* to life. Amen.**

1st STOP DISCOVERY (10 minutes)
Voices and Choices

The human mind cannot process two competing voices. It needs to turn one off in order to hear the other. Facing two opposing beliefs at the same time is called cognitive dissonance. Our kids are faced with this dilemma on a regular basis. Have the children play this game to show them how values can oppose one another.

Have kids form teams of three. Have one child from each team sit in a chair while the other two stand on each side. When you signal them to start, have the two standing kids talk into the ears of the seated child constantly for twenty seconds. Then have the child

Enlarge the sixth commandment on page 10, and make a copy for each child in your class. Have crayons or markers available so children arriving early or leaving late can color and decorate the pages for their notebooks.

TOUR GUIDE TIP
Enlarge the sixth commandment on page 10, and make a copy for each child in your class. Have crayons or markers available so children arriving early or leaving late can color and decorate the pages for their notebooks.

TOUR GUIDE TIP
The activities in this book have been designed for multi-age groups. Select from the activities or adapt them as needed for your class.

in the chair cover one ear and then the other to experiment with isolating the voices. Have the kids switch places until all of them have had a chance to be the hearer.

In their trios, have them discuss the following questions:

• How did you react to having two voices talking to you at the same time?

• How is this like God's voice and the world's voice?

• How can you listen to God's voice?

Say: God gave the sixth commandment loudly and clearly: "You shall not kill." But we live in a world that loves violence. Our movies, TV shows, music, and video games are full of people hurting one another. That's what violence is. God begs you to 🌀 say *no* to violence and *yes* to life. He wants you to hear his voice and make the right choice. God's special people understand that all of life is special to God.

TOUR GUIDE TIP

The Hebrew word for killing (rasah) emphasizes the sanctity of human life. If the kids ask about hunting animals or killing people in war, assure them that God's sixth law does not expressly prohibit these types of bloodshed.

STORY EXCURSION

(15 minutes)

Tugged in Two

Enlarged pictures tell this story of a young boy caught between competing values.

Preparation: Before class, photocopy the "Tugged in Two" handout (page 72). Then cut the pictures apart, and enlarge each one to fill an 8½ x11-inch sheet. If you'd like, you can copy the enlargements onto overhead transparencies and color them.

Items to Pack: enlarged copies of the pictures from the "Tugged in Two" handout, and, for each child, 1 photocopy of the same "Tugged in Two" handout (p. 72), crayons or colored pencils

Give everyone a copy of the "Tugged in Two" handout. As you tell the story, hold the enlarged pictures up (or project transparencies onto a wall or screen), and write appropriate endings for the sentences. The children can color their copies while you tell the story.

(Picture 1) Hans was a happy child. He loved God and wanted to obey God's sixth commandment, "You shall not kill." He learned that watching horror movies and playing violent video games made it seem that human life was worth nothing at all. He decided to 🌀 say *no* to violence and *yes* to life. Then he went to his friend Jeremy's house. (Write the words, "Say no to violence and yes to life," in the balloon on the picture.)

(Picture 2) Jeremy had his own TV, VCR, and Nintendo station in his bedroom. "I can watch and play whatever I want," Jeremy bragged. "Come on, let's play Death Squad."

"Death Squad?" asked Hans. "Isn't that the game where a killer goes around shooting anything and anybody that moves?"

"Yeah," replied Jeremy. "So what?" (Add the words, "Death Squad," to the balloon on this picture.)

(Picture 3) Hans was in a horrible situation. He kind of wanted to play Death Squad, but he was sure God wouldn't be pleased. He wanted to see the action, but he was bothered by the way people were killed as if they had no value. He didn't want Jeremy to think he was a baby, but he knew God's laws were for his good. "What should I do?" he thought. "Maybe I can just watch it and not actually play it," he thought and prayed at the same time. (Ask for suggestions about how Hans might be feeling, and write one suggestion in the balloon for this picture.)

(Picture 4) Hans felt pulled in two different directions. He felt Jeremy and Death Squad pulling him to play the game. What if Jeremy told his other school buddies, "Hans is a sissy. He only likes Toby the Tractor"? If he played this game with Jeremy, they'd be even better friends. Then he felt as if God was pulling his other arm, whispering, ⬤ "Say *no* to violence. I love people. They are precious. Say *yes* to life. Watch something that respects people's lives." (Fill in the first balloon with the words, "Play Death Squad?" and the second with the words, "Say no to violence and yes to life.")

(Picture 5) Hans took a deep breath. He gathered all his courage. He looked Jeremy straight in the eye and said, "I can't play Death Squad. It's full of violence. It shows people getting killed as if they're nothing more than flies."

Jeremy said, "But nobody would know. I'll lock the door so no one can see."

Hans said, "God can see right through walls. He sees everything. He knows what's good for me."

"I guess you're right." Jeremy shrugged his shoulders. (Add the words, "No. That game is full of violence," to the balloon in this picture.)

(Picture 6) Then Hans had a great idea. He thought of something else they could do. "Hey, Jeremy," Hans said, "Why don't you show me that nest of new birds in your backyard? We can see new life."

"Sounds great," Jeremy said. "Let's go!"

Hans smiled up at God, and it felt as if God smiled down at him. (Add the words, "Go see the new life," to the balloon in this picture.)

After the story, have kids form pairs and answer the following questions:
• How did Hans feel in Jeremy's room?
• What did Hans do to ⬤ say *no* to violence?
• What did Hans do to ⬤ say *yes* to life?
• When have you been in a situation like Hans'?
• What can you do the next time you are faced with this problem?

Say: Hans had a problem that each one of you will face over and over again. Ask your parents to help you. It's awfully hard to ⬤ say *no* to violence on your own. Ask your parents to tell your friends and their parents that you are not allowed to watch shows full of terror and violence. If your parents don't, *you* tell your friends right away—before they even turn on the movie—that you're not allowed to watch movies like that. Let's say it together. "I'm not allowed to watch movies like that." It will be very hard to do at times, but God will be pleased with you when you watch shows and play games that respect life.

(15 minutes)
Opposing Paths to Pick

In this activity, the children will create two paths and choose which path to follow.

Items to Pack: blank paper, masking tape, and, for each child, 1 pencil

On each of at least ten pieces of paper, write the name of a currently popular horror movie, TV show, video game, or book that is not God-honoring. Let the children help you name them. Place the papers on the floor to form a path that curves to the left.

For the other path, have the older children write down a different one of the following verses in their own words on each piece of paper: Deuteronomy 30:19; Proverbs 4:17; Proverbs 6:16-17; Matthew 15:19; Philippians 1:27; Philippians 4:8; Colossians 3:2-3; 2 Timothy 4:5a; Hebrews 4:13; 1 Peter 1:13; and 1 Peter 2:9-11. Place the papers on the floor to form a path that curves to the right. Use tape to secure the papers. At the end of that path, tape to the wall a paper that says, "Say *yes* to life."

Have each child tell about a situation in which he or she might be faced with these two paths. Then have them choose the right path, reading some of the verses as they go. For example, a child might say, "When my stepbrother comes for weekends, he always brings this game called Murder Masters. The next time he brings it, I'll say, 'I'm not going to play that because it doesn't respect human life.' "

After each child has had a chance to go down the right path, ask:

• **How did it feel to be faced by two different paths?**

• **When do you feel like this in real life?**

• **How can saying *no* to violence be like saying *yes* to life?**

• **What can you say to your friends when you confront choices like this?**

Say: **Your whole life as a Christian will be a battle between wanting to join the world's side and wanting to please God. But God's laws are really *not* just ten things you may want to follow sometimes. They are commandments. God says, "Do not kill."** ● Say *no* to violence by telling your friends, "I'm not allowed to watch movies like that." Say *yes* to life by having something better to play or watch. Be prepared! It sounds simple, but I know it's not.

SCENIC ROUTE → Provide an enticing alternative for the children in your class. Invite the kids to your home for an evening of wholesome entertainment. Serve special snacks, and show a good Christian movie. Try to rent one from your church library or local Christian bookstore, or ask the kids to bring some of their favorites to share. If available, take a mini "field trip" to your church library to show the kids some videos that are available for them that say yes to life (videos that are not violent).

(20 minutes)
TV (Too Violent) Guide

Kids will learn to discriminate between acceptable movies and those that are too violent.

Preparation: Tape the paper to the wall. At the top, write, "You shall not kill." On the left side write, "Too violent," and on the right side write, "OK to watch or play or read."

Items to Pack: poster board, marker, scissors, glue sticks, several TV Guides (at least 3 for every 10 kids)

Have the kids look through the TV Guides and cut out movie descriptions that sound violent. Some examples include, "*Student Bodies:* Texas teens aim to catch slasher on prom night," and "*Strangers by Night:* Policeman suspects he's a serial killer." Have the children tape these to the left side of the paper. Then have them cut out descriptions of decent movies they'd like to see and tape them to the right side. Have them write in the names of weekly TV shows, popular video games, and books on the appropriate side. Let some volunteers write all over the left side in large letters, "Say *no* to violence" and on the right side, "Say *yes* to life."

Ask:

• **If you were to invite Jesus to sit with you and watch a show, what would you want him to see?**

• **What would you want him to see you seeing?**

• **What movies or video games do you think he wouldn't be pleased with? Why?**

• **How can these movies or games harm you?**

• **What can you do to say *no* to violence and *yes* to life?**

Say: **God tells us to** 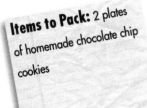 **say *no* to violence. Don't become a part of people harming other people. God tells us to set our minds on things above and to be changed by having a pure mind.** Read Colossians 3:2 and Romans 12:2. **That's how you can say *yes* to life!**

SCENIC ROUTE →

Pass around an uncut TV Guide. Have the kids use bright markers to highlight the shows that God would be pleased to have them watch. Ask them to learn to plan ahead at home to say *yes* to God-honoring shows.

Items to Pack: for each child, 1 photocopy of the "Tugged in Two" handout (p. 72) used in the Story Excursion, pen, crayons

SOUVENIRS → (15 minutes)

My Own Story

The children will write their own stories for this take-home activity.

Preparation: For the nonwriters in your class, fill in the blanks on pictures 1, 4, and 6, according to the directions below. This will save class time.

Have the kids personalize the story by filling in the blanks in the handout's speech balloons. For example, they can fill in the lines of the first and fourth pictures with "Say *no* to violence." In the second picture, they can write the title of a violent video game they are tempted to play. For the third picture, ask them to imagine how they would feel in the situation Hans faced. Children might write, "I'm not allowed to play games like that," in the fifth picture. On the last picture, they can write the name of an alternative activity they would rather do.

Tell the children to be sure to share the handouts with their parents. Ask:

• **What's the hardest thing about** 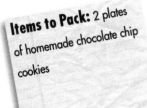 **saying *no* to violence?**

• **How is saying *no* to violence a way of obeying God's law: "You shall not murder"?**

• **How is watching decent movies like saying *yes* to life?**

Say: **When we feel tugged by our friends or older brothers and sisters, it can be very hard to hear God's voice. Pray before you go to friends' homes, and tell your friends and their parents as soon as you get there that you are not allowed to watch movies that have killing in them.**

SCENIC ROUTE →

Have the kids turn their pictures into a book. They can cut out the pictures, glue them to squares of construction paper, and staple the construction paper together. Let them read their stories to one another.

(10 minutes)

Hidden Danger

In this activity, children will learn that things that look appealing can conceal danger.

Preparation: Make the cookies at home, adding some mud to a small portion of one batch.

Set one plate of cookies in front of the children, and say: **I made these myself. I used brown sugar, flour, and vanilla. Everything about these cookies is pure.** Set the "tainted" batch before the children and say: **I made this other plate of cookies, too. I**

Items to Pack: 2 plates of homemade chocolate chip cookies

used the same recipe, but I added one extra ingredient. It was...mud. Just a little bit. Would you like one?

When the kids refuse, ask:

• **Why wouldn't you eat the cookies with mud?**

• **How is a little bit of mud in a cookie like one little murder in a movie?**

• **How can a murder movie harm your mind?**

Say: **One awful murder can stay in your mind for a very long time. God tells us to say** *no* **to violence because he wants us to be pure, just like a pure cookie, baked with the right ingredients. Let's say** *yes* **to life and eat the pure cookies and throw away the rest!**

TRAVEL-ALONG COMMANDMENT SONG (5 minutes)

Teach your kids the following lines and motions. See pages 6-8 to review the song up to this point.

Five fingers for a body, one finger for a sword—*(hold up five fingers on right hand and one on left)*

You shall not kill is the sixth law of the Lord. *("Sword" made from one finger pierces the other hand.)*

Say *no* **to violence in TV and shows.** *(Turn palms outward and push away, like a refusal.)*

Say *yes* **to life. It's the way to go!** *(Nod head. Hands up in a cheer.)*

ONE WAY ▷ (20 minutes)
Faced With Grace

Children will pretend to live a life without rules to understand why God gave us his rules.

Items to Pack: chalkboard and chalk or marker board and markers

Say: **Jarod could act any way he wanted at home. He had no rules. He never had to clear the table. He never had to say, "Excuse me," when he bumped into his little sister. He could yell and be wild when adults were visiting. And then he went to school.** Have the kids list some rules they have at school. Write these on the board. Now let the older kids make up a story about what happens when Jarod goes to school and ignores the school rules. Allow each child to add a part to the story until all of the rules listed on the board have been incorporated into the story. The younger kids can act out the story as it unfolds. For example, an older child may say: "When the teacher asked Jarod to come up to the map and find Florida, Jarod just twirled around in his chair and said, 'I don't feel like it.' Jarod got his name written on the board."

Ask:

• **Why was Jarod's behavior not a problem at home?**

• **Why was his behavior a problem at school?**

• **How are God's commandments like school rules?**

• **How do the commandments show us our sin?**

Have a student read Romans 5:20 from *The Living Bible*: "The Ten Commandments were given so that all could see the extent of their failure to obey God's laws. But the more we see our sinfulness, the more we see God's abounding grace forgiving us."

SCENIC ROUTE

Give each child an inexpensive wooden yardstick. Or you can use wooden paint stirrers and delineate them as rulers. Have the children write on the backs in permanent marker: "God's rules show us our sin. Our sin shows us our need for Jesus, our Savior." Have kids lay the rulers on the floor and jump. Let them measure their jumps and discuss Romans 3:23 about falling short of God's measurements.

Say: **Jarod didn't know he had a problem until he knew he had rules. Rules show us our sin. Our sin shows us our need for a Savior. The more we see our sin, the more grateful we are for God's grace, or his forgiveness. God didn't erase or change the rules. He didn't say, "Well, that's OK!" and ignore our sin. God sent his Son, Jesus, to pay for our sin. That's grace! We break the commandments and God pays for our sin. Isn't God's plan the best?**

HOME AGAIN PRAYER

(5 minutes)

After the kids have prayed the following prayer or one of their own, have them form a circle and put their hands in a pile in the center. End with this cheer: "Two, four, six, eight! Killing is a sin God hates. One, two, three, four, five! I'll say *yes* to life!"

Say: **Dear God, sometimes I'm tempted to watch movies such as** [have each child insert the name of a movie he or she is tempted to watch]. **Please help me to be strong when I'm faced with tough choices. Please give me the strength to say *no* to violence. Please give me the strength to say *yes* to life. Help me to tell my friends that I'm not allowed to watch movies like that. Please remind me! Amen.**

BACK ROAD TO WRITING

(10 minutes)
Leather Vellum

Another material used for recording people's thoughts and ideas was parchment, made from the hides of sheep. First the sheep's wool was removed, then the skin was split into sheets. These sheets were soaked, dried, scraped, dusted, and rubbed smooth. Parchment was Europe's "paper" for a thousand years. Parchment was expensive then, and it still is today, so we will use inexpensive felt to write the sixth commandment on.

1. Cut out the felt so it looks like the shape of an animal hide. (Round the edges and cut a few curves.)

2. Put the briquette in the cup, and pour a little boiling water over it. Use the paintbrush handle to break up and stir the briquette until the water becomes thick and dark. Add a drop or two of oil to the mixture.

3. Paint the commandment onto the felt with the coal/water mixture.

4. Allow the felt to dry. You may want to mount the felt onto a sturdy piece of paper.

Extra Cool

To make this even more realistic, you can purchase material that looks like real leather at a craft store. To make it look like drying animal skin, sew it to a frame made from chopsticks. You may want to use permanent or fabric marker to write the commandment. (See the picture.)

- -
Did You Know?
Did you know that the churches and monasteries kept reading and writing alive in the Dark Ages? Monks were men who lived apart from others and devoted their lives to God. The monks very carefully copied the Bible onto parchment. They worked hours, days, months, and years on end to make copies of the Bible. They couldn't even use candles for light because of the fear that their precious work might catch on fire.
- -

Items to Pack: boiling water, olive or vegetable oil, and, for each child, 1 charcoal briquette, 1 piece of tan-colored felt, paintbrush, scissors, cup

FUN FACT Parchment was expensive, but it lasted longer than papyrus, which was more likely to crumble as it aged. Parchment was first rolled into scrolls. Later it was cut into sheets and sewn into books. A very special type of parchment, called "vellum," was made from the skins of antelopes or calves. It was softer and took the ink marks well. It took the skins of more than three hundred sheep to make a Bible!

FUN FACT Because of all the work necessary to make the skins and ink, and to copy and bind books, parchment and vellum books were extremely expensive. In fact, books were chained up in libraries so no one would steal them. This also assured that the books wouldn't be placed somewhere where mold, mice, and bookworms might destroy them.

71

Tugged in Two

Dear Mom and Dad:

This story reminds me of myself when _____

_____

Please help me to help myself say *no* to violence and *yes* to life. Please tell my friends that I'm not allowed to watch violent or horror movies. Thank you for helping me.

JOURNEY 8

The Seventh Commandment:
Be True to Your Husband or Wife

Pathway Point: 🌐 Keep your promises.

In-Focus Verse: "You shall not commit adultery" (Exodus 20:14).

Travel Itinerary

We know that many American husbands and wives break God's commandment, "You shall not commit adultery." In the debris of this cataclysmic devastation are the children in broken homes asking, "Why don't Mommy and Daddy live together anymore?" or "Why does Daddy have a girlfriend?"

A lifetime can be a very long time to stay faithful to one person. Is God asking too much? How is the seventh commandment relevant to children? While children can't control their parents, they are never too young to learn the concepts behind God's commandments, even adult issues such as this one. By focusing on what children do understand (broken promises), you can help children to appreciate a God who asks the grown-ups in their world to keep their vows. It's never too early to teach children God's ways. As God's values are reinforced, they become a vital part of children, affecting their choices throughout their lives.

DEPARTURE PRAYER (5 minutes)

Teach the children a lesson that can change their lives. Teach them to "pray the Bible." Write the words of Exodus 20:14 on the board or on newsprint, and then write our version of the commandment, "Be true to your husband or wife." Ask the children to keep their eyes open, and have one of the older children point to the words while you pray them. Finish with the following words, or choose your own.

Say: **Dear Lord our God, you are true to us. You keep all of your promises. Please help us to keep all of our promises, too. When we grow up, help us to always be true to our husbands or wives. Help us understand what that truly means. You are a good and loving God. You stick by us no matter what. Help us learn to become people who always keep our promises. We want you to be proud of us. Amen.**

1st STOP DISCOVERY (15 minutes)
Sticking With You

In this activity, the children will learn the importance of keeping their promises.

Have children form pairs. Tell them that one partner in each pair will think of something for the other partner to do while crossing the room. This will be the promise to be kept. Then the pair will cross the room with their arms linked. The rules

TOUR GUIDE TIP

Enlarge the seventh commandment on page 10, and make a copy for each child in your class. Have crayons or markers available so children arriving early or leaving late can color and decorate the pages for their notebooks.

TOUR GUIDE TIP

Some kindergartners are confused by the terms "husband" and "father" since they rarely hear their dads referred to in these ways. To clarify these terms, show children a picture of a family, and tell them the titles of each person in the family. Then give the children magazines containing pictures of families, and let the children give each family member's various titles.

TOUR GUIDE TIP

Teach children the scriptural wording of this commandment: "You shall not commit adultery." Define the words "commit" and "adultery" for the children, but avoid a heavy discussion about sex. You may want to explain that adultery is falling in love with a person one is not married to. If older children ask you questions about sex that are inappropriate for little ones, ask those kids to talk to their parents.

The activities in this book have been designed for multi-age groups. Select from the activities or adapt them as needed for your class.

are (1) they must keep arms linked the whole time, (2) they must go the entire length of the room and back, and (3) they must keep their promise the whole way there and back.

For example, one partner might tell the other partner to quack like a duck while they cross the room. The performing partner would respond by saying, "I promise to stick with you even if I have to quack like a duck." Then the partners walk across the room while the performing partner quacks like a duck. Then partners switch roles. When that pair has finished, another pair practices promise-keeping.

When all the kids have had a turn, ask:

- **How did you feel as you crossed the room?**
- **How is keeping your promise like obeying the seventh commandment?**
- **What do you need to remember when you grow up and get married?**

Say: **Some of you felt silly keeping your promises; some of you were embarrassed. But you all kept your promises! God asks us to keep promises no matter how we feel. God is very serious about a husband being true to his wife and a wife being true to her husband. When you grow up, your husband or wife may not ask you to do silly things, but he or she will ask you to love only him or her for the rest of your life! Let's get serious about keeping our promises!**

STORY EXCURSION *(15 minutes)* A Better Offer

In this story, a child promises to go to a birthday party but then gets a better offer. What will he do? As you read the story, pause when you reach bracketed text, allowing the kids to fill in the blanks. Kids can come up with their own ideas, or you can suggest the ones we've supplied.

Say: **When Mr. Spencer wrote the seventh commandment on the board** ["Be true to your husband or wife."], **Caleb checked out. As he made paper planes, he thought, "I don't have to listen now. I don't have a wife, and I don't want one when I grow up."**

Mr. Spencer walked over to Caleb. Towering over him, he looked down at Caleb and said, "Of course, you all know this commandment means that ["we need to keep our promises"]. **Caleb put his paper airplanes away.**

On Tuesday, when he got home, Caleb threw his backpack on the table and raced to answer the phone. "Yeah, cool, I'll be there. Wait a minute..." Caleb called his mom to the phone. "Mom, come talk to Alec's mom. Alec has a great birthday party planned this Friday night."

After she had talked to Alec's mom, Caleb's mom said, "Sounds like fun. And you're the only one invited to the party."

"Yeah, I get to [sleep over and go fishing the next day]**!"**

Caleb's mom said, "I'm sure it means a lot to Alec that you can celebrate his birthday with him, especially since he [doesn't have a brother or sister and since he's new to our area]**."**

Caleb and his dad went out the next day to buy a present for Alec. Caleb explained to his dad, "We have to make this a super-special gift since I'll be the only one at the party!"

First they went to a store called [Wal-mart], but they didn't find anything there. So they went to [Toys A Million] and found the perfect gift. It was a [Space Alien Lab]. Caleb came home and wrapped it in newspaper comics. To make the package look more special, he added a [big swirl lollipop].

In school the next day, Alec said, "Hey, Caleb, when you spend the night we can [sleep in a tent in the backyard]." Caleb promised to be there.

On Thursday, Caleb's mom handed him an invitation. It was from [name], Caleb's best friend. [Name] was having a sleepover party the same night as Alec's party, and the next day the party guests were going to Caleb's favorite place [Action Odyssey]. The more Caleb thought about missing out on the action, the angrier he felt about being stuck at Alec's house. "Oh, man," thought Caleb, "I'll just tell Alec that [I'll come to his house another night]." He picked up the phone. Before he could dial Alec's number, these words came back to him: "Keep your promises. Keep your promises."

Caleb picked up the phone. He put it down. He picked up the phone. He put it down. "What are you doing?" his dad asked.

"I'm thinking of calling Alec and telling him I can't go to his party," Caleb said.

"Why can't you?" his dad asked.

Caleb handed him the invitation to [name]'s party. "I see," his dad said. "You got a better offer. This is a big choice for you. You need to learn now to keep your promises. What if I got a better offer for a wife? There are a lot of friendly, smart women at my office."

"What does that have to do with...Come on, dad, that's a stretch."

"Not really, Caleb," his dad continued. "God commanded me to be true to my wife. I made a promise to do that. It's all about keeping promises, even when we don't feel like it."

"OK," Caleb sighed. "Deep down, I knew I needed keep my promise to Alec."

Caleb went to Alec's party. They had a blast. They [ate popcorn, jumped on his trampoline, and caught polliwogs in the creek]. Caleb had so much fun that he never even thought about the other party. Later, Alec wrote Caleb a thank-you note that read, "[Thanks for making my birthday the best I've ever had]!"

Caleb thought about God and his ways. He thought, "Yep, it's all about keeping your promises. I'm glad I kept my promise to Alec."

Thank the children for their help. Ask:

• What was the better offer that Caleb got?

• How does this remind you of God's seventh commandment, "Be true to your husband or wife"?

• Has it ever been hard for you to keep a promise? Tell about it.

Say: Keeping promises can be tough. Sometimes we have to say no to things we really like. It's good to 🌐 keep your promises. Build your promise-keeping muscles now so that you can be true to your husband or wife when you grow up.

Items to Pack: index cards, pencils, and, for the groom, a man's suit jacket (with a flower pinned on for effect), and, for the bride, a veil (an inexpensive piece of white material will do) and/or bouquet

ADVENTURE IN LIVING GOD'S LAWS

(15 minutes)
Wedding to Wake

This funny, active game reinforces the concept that marriage is a lifelong commitment.

Preparation: Prepare an index card for each child in your class. Write on all the cards, "I promise to be true to you until..." On each card, complete the sentence with a different one of the following statements: "I find someone I like better," "I find someone who makes more money," "I get tired of you," "I don't care about you anymore," "I fall in love with someone else," "I find someone who is better looking," "I meet someone who is nicer," "I find someone who is smarter," and "death us do part."

Arrange the chairs to create an aisle, as in a traditional church. Ask the children to be seated, being sure to seat nonreaders next to readers. Hand each child a card, facedown.

Say: **In a wedding ceremony, the bride and groom agree to keep their promises until they die. They use the words "until death us do part." That means they promise to stay true to each other and not to fall in love with anyone else as long as they are both alive. Let's see which of you received the card with the promise God wants married people to keep.**

Ask children to read their cards aloud. The child who reads, "death us do part" gets to be the bride or groom. Dress the child as either the bride or the groom, and let him or her walk down the aisle. Then shuffle the cards and redistribute them. Play the game until everyone gets a chance to be the bride or groom. Then have the kids form pairs or trios to discuss the following questions:

• **How was this game like a real wedding?**
• **Which card had the only promise that would please God?**
• **Why is it important for you to learn about being true in marriage?**

Say: **A wedding is a happy day. The bride and groom say, "I promise to be true to you until death." They mean it. But life is hard, and there are times when it's hard to keep our promises to our partners. That's when we remember that it is God himself who *commands* us, "You shall not commit adultery."**

(15 minutes)
Verse to Live Happily Ever After

In this activity, team members will race to phrase a verse in their own words.

Items to Pack: Bible, bell

Form two teams, the Husbands and the Wives. Set a bell across the room. Read a Scripture verse about marriage from the following list or others you know: Genesis 2:24a; Proverbs 6:32; Matthew 19:5; Matthew 19:6; Ephesians 5:25; and Ephesians 5:33. After you have read a verse, have a husband go with a wife to the bell. The first one to ring the bell gets to put the verse into his or her own words. Then have the other child do the same.

After everyone has had a chance, ask:

• **What promise does God ask husbands and wives to keep?**
• **What promises do you keep?**
• **What would you like to ask me about this commandment?**

Say: God's plan hasn't changed. He still wants husbands and wives to stay true to each other. Learn to keep your promises, and you will be able to stay true to your husband or wife when you grow up. God chose you to be among his special people who keep their promises.

 **(15 minutes)**
Path of Promise

In this activity, partners will work together to negotiate a pathway of compromising choices.

Have the children find partners. One child will sit in front of his or her paper. This child has to listen to the directions of his or her partner to draw a line from the beginning of the maze at the picture of the foot to the end of the maze at the picture of the goal. To accomplish this, the other partner will stand behind the sitting partner, covering the seated partner's eyes. The standing partner will give directions to his or her partner, encouraging the partner to stay on the path of commitment that leads to the goal. Then the partners will switch so the other child can complete the maze in the same manner. Have each child write the words, "Keep your promises," on the path. Using marker, have the children highlight and read aloud the benefits of sticking out the season.

Ask:

• **What did you have to do to stay on the path of promise?**

• **How is staying on the path like keeping all your promises?**

• **Can you share about a time you made a commitment and didn't want to keep it?**

Say: God is pleased when you keep your promises. Besides being proud of yourself, you are also practicing being a promise-keeper. As you grow, God expects you to ⬤ keep your promises, especially if you get married. When you keep your promises, you are a winner!

 **(5 minutes)**

Teach the children this new stanza and accompanying motions. See pages 6-8 to review the song up to this point.

Be true to your husband. Be true to your wife. *(Hold up one finger on each hand.)*

Keep your promises all your life. *(Hook fingers together.)*

God told people, "I want to be obeyed. *(Hold up index finger.)*

Remember those promises that you made!" *(Point index finger forward.)*

 **(20 minutes)**
Broken Promises, Broken Savior

Broken pretzel sticks serve as a reminder of our sin of broken promises to God.

Hold up a pretzel. Say: **When two people marry, they promise to be true to each other. If one of them breaks his or her promise, their relationship** (use the word "love" for younger children) **is broken.** Break the pretzel. Hold up another pretzel. **In the same way, we promise to keep God's commandments. But when we break a commandment** (break the pretzel), **we have broken our friendship with God** (Isaiah 59:2).

Give each child ten pretzels. List the ten commandments, encouraging children to help you name them. As they list each commandment, ask if they've broken it. If they have, have them each break a pretzel and put the broken pretzels on their plates.

Say: **Here we have a mess, a pile of sins and broken friendship with God.** Hold up two pretzels that haven't been broken. **But there are two pieces of wood that remind us of how this whole mess can be fixed.** Form the two pretzels into a cross. **Jesus came to die for our sins. His body was broken on two pieces of wood because of our broken promises. When you say you are sorry for your sins and believe in him** (form a continuous line out of the two pretzel sticks), **you come back into a loving friendship with God. God sweeps away all your sins.** Hand each child a fresh pretzel as a token of a renewed relationship with God.

Ask:

• **What happens when we sin?**

• **What can we do about it?**

• **Have you ever asked Jesus to sweep away all your sins?**

Use this time to talk individually with the children who have more questions while other students munch on their pretzels.

Items to Pack: 1 pretzel stick for each child

HOME AGAIN PRAYER

(5 minutes)

Have the kids sit in a circle and hold their pretzels in front of them. Tell them this shows how their friendship with one another is whole if they keep their promises to one another. Give each of the children an opportunity to pray aloud. Tell them to take their pretzels home as reminders to "stick" by their promises.

Say: **Dear Jesus, thank you for coming to die for us. Thank you for sweeping our sins away. Thank you for wanting to be our friend. You are amazing and wonderful. Please teach us how we can keep our promises. Because we love you we want to please you. Amen.**

BACK ROAD TO WRITING

(15 minutes)
Movable Type

Another development in the way people recorded their thoughts and ideas happened in China. The people there learned to carve their symbols into wood, cover the wood with ink, and press the wood onto a piece of paper. A whole piece of wood was carved for each page they wanted to print. This block printing was very slow because they needed to carve an entire block for each page. Then a man named Pi Sheng came up with a simple but important discovery: Individual pieces of wood containing only one symbol could be arranged and rearranged within a frame to print a page. Simulate this method by printing the seventh commandment with a type of moveable blocks, an alphabet stamp set. (For nonreaders, write the commandment on paper, and let them stamp right on top of your letters.)

1. Brush paint on the letter B with a paintbrush, and press it onto a sheet paper.

2. Continue in this way, using all the letters in the commandments, until you have printed, "Be true to you husband or wife."

3. Let the paper dry.

Did You Know?

Did you know that Johannes Gutenberg, a German, was one of history's most important inventors? He developed the printing press and movable type made out of steel and brass. For the first time in history, many pages could quickly be printed exactly the same as the others. The first book Gutenberg printed was the Bible. The Bible has been and still is the best-selling book in the world.

Did You Know?

Did you know why we call capital letters "uppercase" and small letters "lowercase"? When letters were developed for use in the printing press, the small letters were placed in a box or case below the capital letters so that they were easier to grab since they were used more often; thus, uppercase and lowercase. Most print was done in uppercase before it was discovered that more letters could be squeezed onto a page using lowercase letters.

Items to Pack: alphabet stamp set, washable tempera paint, paintbrush, paper, water and soap for washing up

FUN FACT If you don't have a set of letter stamps, you can make stamps out of thin craft foam. Cut out the letters, and glue each one to the bottom of a foam cup. For letters that are not symmetrical, such as B, glue them on backward.

FUN FACT The Chinese developed a new printing material— much less costly than parchment— in A.D. 105. However, this invention didn't reach Europe until around A.D. 1150. The paper that a Chinese man named Ts'ai Lun developed was made from the pulp of mulberry bark, rags, and even old fishnets. When he brought it to the emperor, the emperor was so impressed that he ordered Ts'ai Lun to teach this process to other Chinese men.

Path of Promise

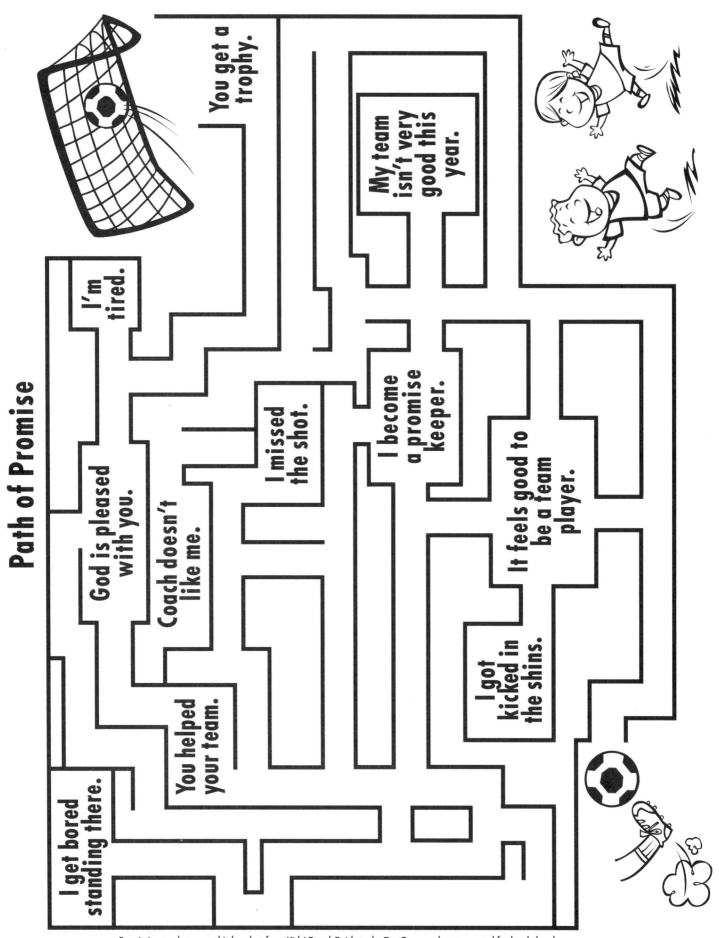

- You get a trophy.
- My team isn't very good this year.
- I'm tired.
- I become a promise keeper.
- I missed the shot.
- God is pleased with you.
- It feels good to be a team player.
- Coach doesn't like me.
- I got kicked in the shins.
- You helped your team.
- I get bored standing there.

JOURNEY 9

The Eighth Commandment:
You Shall Not Steal

Pathway Point: 🌑 Be givers, not getters.

In-Focus Verse: "You shall not steal" (Exodus 20:15).

Travel Itinerary

Children steal quite naturally, even though they know innately that stealing is wrong. It's only when they are clearly taught the four simple words that God carved into stone—"You shall not steal"—that children begin to assimilate this value as their own. Robbery comes in various shades—cheating, defrauding, and borrowing something and failing to return it, for example. God condemns them all.

God not only asks us to refrain from stealing, but he also calls the Christian to earn money so that "he may have something to share with those in need" (Ephesians 4:28). In this lesson, the children will learn to focus on being givers, not getters. They'll practice giving a tithe to the Lord and play a game to see how we can sometimes rationalize our actions. The children will come to understand that God says, "You shall not steal," for very good reasons!

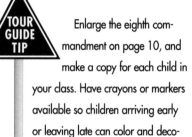

TOUR GUIDE TIP Enlarge the eighth commandment on page 10, and make a copy for each child in your class. Have crayons or markers available so children arriving early or leaving late can color and decorate the pages for their notebooks.

TOUR GUIDE TIP The activities in this book have been designed for multi-age groups. Select from the activities or adapt them as needed for your class.

DEPARTURE PRAYER (5 minutes)

Encourage the children to express open, giving hearts by opening their hands slowly as they say this prayer with you. Pause after each sentence so children can repeat it after you.

Say: **Dear Lord, my God, you give me everything I need and more. You give me food, clothes, and a family. You give me friends, a church, and love. Please help me to never dishonor you by stealing. Help me to become a giver and not a getter. Help me to have open hands, not hands that sneak and take things. I want to be known as one of your special people. Thank you for making me one of your treasures! Amen.**

1st STOP DISCOVERY (15 minutes)
Who, Me? Steal?

The children will talk about different types of stealing.

Count out five pieces of candy for each child. Read each scenario to the group and then ask the following questions. Have the kids repeat the commandment, "You shall not steal." Then they can each eat a piece of candy.

Scenarios:

• **Mandy wanted Chastity's bracelet that she found in Chastity's yard. She looked around and put it in her pocket, telling herself, "I'll call Chastity later and tell her**

Items to Pack: bag of Tootsie Rolls or gum

that I found her bracelet." Mandy never called Chastity. She only wore the bracelet to church. Chastity didn't go to her church.

• Caleb borrowed his brother Jacob's backpack to take to their dad's house for the weekend. When he was there, he ripped it by mistake, ruining it. When his brother complained he just said, "I said I was sorry. Man, what am I supposed to do?"

• David forgot all about the spelling test. He just couldn't get another D or he'd be grounded. When his teacher left the room, David stood up and looked at Katlyn's paper. She always got A's. This time he did too.

• Lauren's little sister always left her money lying around the house. Lauren found the five dollars that her sister got for her birthday and put it in her own piggy bank. "I just found it lying around. She doesn't care about it," Lauren told herself.

Questions:

• Has anything like that ever happened to you?

• How does that break God's commandment, "You shall not steal"?

• What could the person do to be a giver, not a getter?

After the kids have discussed the last scenario, say: **God spoke four simple words in his eighth commandment: "You shall not steal."** God not only tells us not to steal, he also tells us all through the Bible to 🕑 be givers and not getters. As God's special people, we need to be honest in all we do.

Encourage the kids to give a few pieces of candy away to others in the class or to save some for a brother or sister.

STORY EXCURSION (15 minutes)
The Card Shark

Tell this story-poem as you lead kids in a card game.

Preparation: Photocopy the "Sea Monstroids" cards (page 88) onto card stock for each student.

Items to Pack: for each child, 1 photocopy of the "Sea Monstroid" cards (p. 88), scissors, plastic sandwich bag

Give each child a copy of the "Sea Monstroid" cards. Have them each cut the page into individual cards. They'll use these later for a Souvenir. As you read the poem, have the kids hold up each card you mention.

Say: Card Shark had all the Monstroid cards
He could collect, but one was really hard
To find in a trade or anywhere:
The SeaSerSpit card was super-rare.
"I want SeaSerSpit!" Card Shark would shout.
But no one had them, and the stores were sold out.
Card Shark fretted and fumed and fussed and frowned
Until one day, guess what he found.
Five-year-old Tommy had the SeaSerSpit!
Card Shark growled, "It's not *his* favorite!"

"I don't want to give. I want to get, get, get.

"Just watch, I'll get SeaSerSpit yet!"

With jaws open wide, he began to drool.

"I'll get that card. Little kids are such fools."

"Tommy," Card Shark said, with his arm on Tommy's shoulder,

I'll trade you any ten cards in my Monstroid holder."

"No way," Tommy said. "No trade. No deal."

So Card Shark thought of a way to steal.

He looked at the "10" on an Octopoid

And changed it to "40"—that human Monstroid!

"40 points?" Tommy asked. "OK, here's your card."

Card Shark left, and he grinned, back in his yard.

"Wow, what a rip!" Card Shark rejoiced.

Until he heard a quiet voice.

"Be a giver, not a getter. Do not steal," the Lord said.

Now Card Shark had a fight inside his head.

"Here, Tommy," Card Shark gave SeaSerSpit back.

But Tommy had one from his new Monstroid pack.

"Just keep it," Tommy said. And Card Shark smiled.

Keeping God's commandments can be tough, but wild.

Card Shark gave Tommy Sluggo and StingerCray.

They became friends starting that very day.

Have the kids put their cards into a plastic bag and ask:

• What did Card Shark want? What did he do to get it?

• Can you share about a time you wanted something that badly?

• What caused Card Shark to return the card?

Say: Card Shark cheated by changing the "10" to a "40." This is one way to steal, but God says, "No. Be completely honest." We are God's special people, his precious treasure. So we need to show the world how to 🌑 be givers, not getters. It's the best way to obey God's eighth commandment: "You shall not steal."

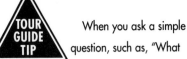

TOUR GUIDE TIP

When you ask a simple question, such as, "What did Card Shark want?" call on the kindergartners. This allows the younger kids a chance to answer when they can. It also teaches the older kids to be sensitive to the younger ones.

SCENIC ROUTE →

You can tell (or retell) this story another way. Have all the kids stand in a circle and link arms. Choose someone to be the Card Shark, and have the youngest child be Tommy. Have Tommy sit in the middle of the circle, playing with his cards. Have the Card Shark "swim" in and out of the kids' linked arms. Then during his discussion with Tommy in the story, have Card Shark swim to the center and act out the story. Have the kids in the circle sway to the rhythm. Get a good beat going before beginning the story.

ADVENTURE IN LIVING GOD'S LAWS

(15 minutes)
Oops, I Just Borrowed It

In this activity, children will watch out for forgery and learn that not returning things is like stealing.

Have the children each draw a picture of a tree. Tell children to make the pictures the best they have ever drawn, but not to write their names on them. When they have finished, collect the pictures, and show them to the class. Then randomly return the pictures facedown. Have the kids turn over the pictures you gave them and sign their names on them, even though the pictures are not theirs. Then have the original artists find their own pictures and take them.

Items to Pack: paper, pencils

Ask:

- How did you feel when you saw someone else's name on your picture?
- How was this experience like stealing?

Say: **Pretending that something you borrowed is your own is also a form of stealing. Sometimes we simply forget to return things to people. God says, "You shall not steal." This means that as God's special people, we need to make sure that what we do can't be interpreted as stealing. Have you ever borrowed something from someone and forgotten to return it? In learning to be givers and not getters, we also need to be returners. Turn your picture over, and write a prayer telling God in what way you want to be a giver this week. Then next week tell the class how you ⬤ were a giver, not a getter!** Have the kids erase the incorrect signatures and write their own.

Items to Pack: for every child, 10 pennies, 1 photocopy of the "One Hundred" chart (p. 89), resealable plastic bag

(15 minutes)
Will You Rob God?

In this activity, the children will learn that it's never too early to learn about tithing.

Preparation: Photocopy the "One Hundred" chart (page 89), enlarging it as much as you'd like.

Give ten pennies to each student. Say: **It was bad enough that the Card Shark tried to steal from a little child, but there is someone who it is even worse to steal from.**

Ask:

- Who would it be even worse to steal from?

Say: **Every day, millions of people all around the world steal from God. Listen to what the prophet Malachi said in the last book of the Old Testament.** Read Malachi 3:8-10.

Ask:

- How did the people rob God?

Say: **The people were robbing God by giving him their leftovers. Everything we have comes from God. Can you imagine stealing from God?**

Have children form pairs. Tell children that they will each get a chance to count their blessings from God by touching a penny for each thing God has given them.

Say: **God wants us to ⬤ be givers, not getters. God asks only for us to give back to him 10 percent. That means for every ten pennies we have, he asks for only one penny back. That's not much, is it?**

Teach the kids what 10 percent is by using the number chart and pennies. Have them work in their pairs to lay pennies on the chart. Explain that 10 percent is one penny from each row of pennies that they cover. Let the older kids figure out how much 10 percent would be from a dollar, fifty cents, and so on. Then collect one penny from each child, and give it to the church fund. Commend the kids who choose to contribute more than one penny. Then have them each put the rest of their pennies in a resealable plastic bag to take home.

SOUVENIRS (20 minutes)
Card Sharks

In this activity, kids will play an action game with their cards to learn how to be givers, not getters.

Preparation: Give each child a set of "Sea Monstroids" cards. (If you didn't do the "Card Shark" activity, photocopy the "Sea Monstroids" cards (page 88) onto card stock, making a set for each child. Have the kids cut them apart. Some early kindergartners may need help.)

Items to Pack: for every child, 1 set of "Sea Monstroids" cards (p. 88), scissors, crayons, plastic sandwich bag

Use this activity to teach the kids how people rationalize before they steal. Have children sit in a circle. Have them place their cards facedown in front of them.

Say: **The Card Shark wanted Tommy's SeaSerSpit card, so he told himself something to make it seem OK that he was stealing Tommy's card. Do you remember what it was? He told himself, "SeaSerSpit is not *his* favorite card." This is a dangerous game people play. We call it rationalizing. Every time you hear Card Shark give a reason he thinks it's OK to steal, put one of your cards into a new pile in front of you further into the middle of the circle.**

Read the following lines:

Tommy has so many cards; he wouldn't miss one.

Tommy doesn't care about SeaSerSpit like I do.

His mom buys his cards for him. I have to work to pay for my own.

I'll give it back later.

Tommy bent my FangGang card anyway.

He's just a little kid. He won't notice if I rip him off.

I deserve that card. I've looked everywhere for it.

When the game is finished, have the kids turn over their last card. Whoever has the Commandment Card is the winner. Have the kids put their cards in a plastic bag to take home. Let them create their own Sea Monstroid on the Commandment Card.

TOUR GUIDE TIP

Coloring takes up valuable class time. If you are short on time, ask the kids to color some projects at home. However, some kids in your class may be kinesthetic learners who actually process detail better while doodling. If coloring helps them to listen to stories and instructions better, let them do it.

TRAVEL-ALONG COMMANDMENT SONG (5 minutes)

Teach the kids this new stanza and the accompanying motions. See pages 6-8 to review up to this point.

Ten take away two is eight. *(Hold up both hands, fingers spread apart. Then one hand "steals" two fingers from the other hand.)*

Stealing is a sin God hates. *(Shake head as you hold both hands at sides.)*

Try to be givers, not gimmie-gimmie getters. *(Hold hands out, then pull them in.)*

Don't be an eighth commandment forgetter. *(Shake a warning finger.)*

ONE WAY (15 minutes)
Over Our Heads

In this activity kids will use yarn to show that no one can attain God's holy standards.

Items to Pack: piece of yarn 1 or 2 yards long

Have two kids hold the yarn about one foot off the ground. They will be raising the yarn after each statement. Be careful that no one trips on the yarn. Say: **God says, "Do** not steal." **If you have never broken into a house and stolen something, step over this line.** After children have stepped over the yarn, have the children holding the yarn raise it to two feet. **God tells us not to rob him. If you have always given God 10 percent of your money, step over the line.** Have the children holding the yarn raise the yarn again to about 3 feet. **God tells us to share with those in need. If you have always shared everything you have with those in need, step over this high line.** Have the kids hold the line over their heads. **No one is able to obey God completely. We are all thieves in some way. Listen to what will happen to thieves:** (Read the following based on 1 Corinthians 6:9-10) **People who are greedy or steal or rob will not share in the kingdom of God.**

So now we have a problem. **God gives us laws that are higher than we are. If we can't obey them, we won't be in God's kingdom. Is our situation hopeless? No! Listen to this:** (Read the following based on Philippians 2:6-11. As you do, have the two kids slowly lower the string until it's lying on the floor. Add another piece to form a cross.) **Jesus was king in heaven. But he didn't stay up on his throne. He left heaven and came down to earth to live as a man. He knew how desperately we needed him. He made himself as nothing and even died a painful death on the cross. Because he died on the cross, our sins can be forgiven. We can be in his kingdom. One day we'll bow with the whole earth and say, "Jesus Christ is Lord!"**

Jesus provides the way for us to step over the line into fellowship with God.

HOME AGAIN PRAYER

(5 minutes)

Have the kids step over the yarn as you read this prayer.

Dear Lord Jesus, thank you for leaving your home in heaven. Thank you for becoming one of us. Thank you for suffering. I know you did it for us. It was our sin that put you on the cross and God's power that caused you to burst out of the tomb. All of us have sinned. All of us have stolen in big ways or little ways. Please help us to obey God's eighth commandment, "You shall not steal." We want to be givers, not getters. We love you. Amen.

BACK ROAD TO WRITING

(10 minutes)
Colonial Kids

In colonial times in America, the children used special books, called hornbooks, to learn to read. A hornbook was a thin piece of wood with a handle and a "page" on each side. Hornbooks got their name from the thin sheet of cow's horn that covered the page to protect it. The children could read right through the transparent cow's horn. The children wrote with goose-quill pens dipped into ink. Let your kids paint the eighth commandment onto wood with a feather.

1. Dip the feather into the paint.
2. Paint the commandment on the wood.
3. Let it dry overnight.

Items to Pack: washable tempera paint, and, for each child, craft feather, thin piece of wood no larger than 8x10 inches with a handle. You can remove the staples from a paddle ball toy, or you can often find lightweight wooden cutting boards to use. Some dollar stores sell oven shovels that are an almost-perfect imitation of a hornbook.

Did You Know?

Colonial children didn't have paper to write on because it was still expensive and hard to come by. The kids would go into the woods and peel the bark off trees to write on. They would make their ink out of the juice of berries. Sometimes they would burn a stick and use the charred end of the stick to write with.

Extra Cool

You could pretend to be a colonial kid. You can use a piece of charcoal to scratch a verse onto paper or wood. Charcoal sticks can be purchased in art stores, or you can find charred, or burned, pieces of wood.

FUN FACT

Students in Colonial times spent a lot of time learning how to have handsome handwriting. In public school they would write the Lord's Prayer and Bible verses. However, the teachers weren't concerned with proper spelling. Once a schoolteacher advertised in a newspaper that he taught "writeing AND spilling"!

Sea Monstroids

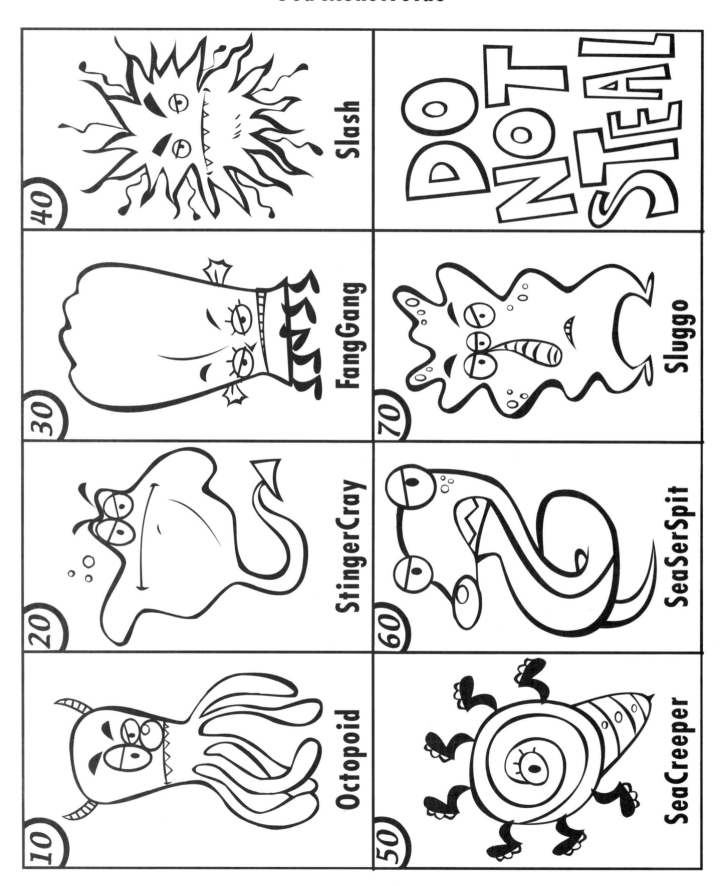

One Hundred

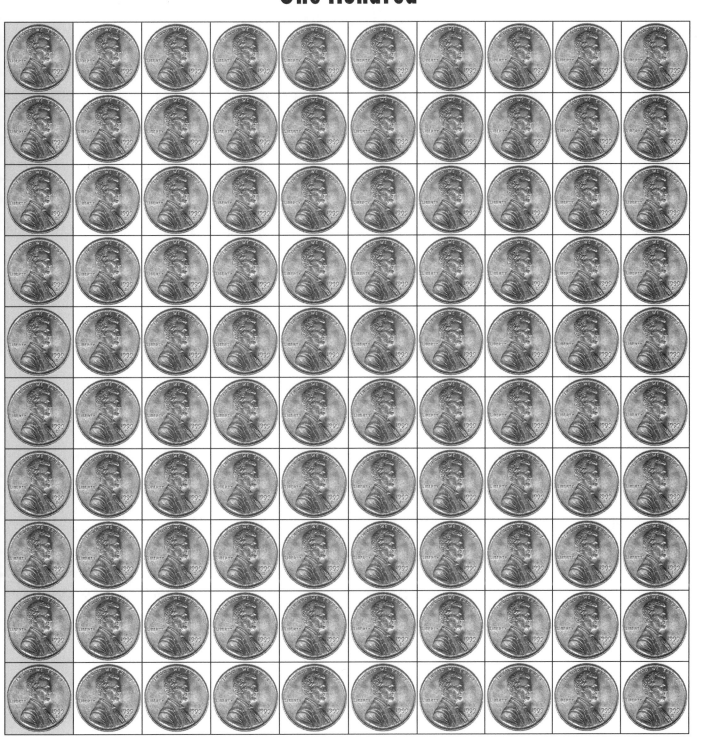

The Ninth Commandment:
You Shall Not Lie

Pathway Point: 🌐 Always tell the truth.

In-Focus Verse: "You shall not give false testimony against your neighbor" (Exodus 20:16).

Travel Itinerary

My two-year-old's answer to "Where are my car keys?" was "The big, bad wolf came in and ate them all up." You don't need to teach a child how to lie. Lying is a latent part of our human nature. In Genesis alone there are at least eleven stories of people who lied and/or deceived. And that's only the first book! From Abraham to Ananias, the entire Bible is full of God's people lying, deceiving, and bending the truth. People lie mostly out of fear of other people. It's not other people we ought to fear but our holy God who commands, "You shall not give false testimony."

It's logical that God prohibits lying after he forbids stealing. We often lie to cover up other sins. In this lesson, the children will see who is hurt by lies; see what messes come from our lies; learn that it's always best to tell the truth, even though they may suffer consequences; and commit themselves to truth-telling.

TOUR GUIDE TIP Enlarge the ninth commandment on page 10, and make a copy for each child in your class. Have crayons or markers available so children arriving early or leaving late can color and decorate the pages for their notebooks.

TOUR GUIDE TIP The activities in this book have been designed for multi-age groups. Select from the activities or adapt them as needed for your class.

DEPARTURE PRAYER (10 minutes)

It's often hard for children to realize that they are talking to a real being when they pray since they can't see or feel God. To give your kids a glimmer of the reality of our God, who hears and answers prayers, ask them to share about times God has answered their prayers. Go back through the prayers from previous journeys, and write them on the board. Discuss any changes the children have seen that show them that God is shaping them into his special people and hearing their prayers.

Dear Lord, please help us to be truth-tellers. Help us to stop lying. We are sorry for all the lies we've told. You told us you are the Truth. Lord, we want to be truth-tellers to show we are your followers. Help us to know in our minds and hearts that it's always best to tell the truth. Amen.

Items to Pack: dowel or stick, yarn, magnet, construction paper, scissors, paper clips, small individual prizes such as gum or stickers

1st STOP DISCOVERY (20 minutes)
Wishing and Fishing

In this activity, children will go fishing, wish for a prize, and contrast honesty to being lied to.

Preparation: From construction paper, cut at least as many fish as you have students, and attach a paper clip to each. On the back of the fish write, "You win!" Make a fishing pole from the dowel, yarn, and magnet. Turn the fish word-side down.

Set up a fishing game. Say: **Each of you will get a turn to hook a fish. Try to hook a fish that says, "You win!" on it.**

Give each child a chance to hook a fish. You may want to set up two stations if you have a large class. Give the children who hooked a "You win!" fish a prize. Let them sit down. The rest of the class will fish until each child hooks a "You win!" fish.

Ask:

• **How did you feel when you hooked a fish that said, "You win!"?**

• **How would you feel if you hadn't ever hooked a winning fish?**

Say: **Did you know that at some fairs, there are people who lie to children? They set up games and say it's easy to win, but actually, no one can win. In a game like this, not one fish would say, "You win!" even though they tell the children that one fish says, "You win!"**

Ask:

• **What do you call something that isn't the truth?**

• **Have you ever been lied to? How did it feel?**

• **Why do you think God says in his ninth commandment, "You shall not lie"?**

Say: **We feel awful when someone lies to us. God wants us to tell the truth so much that he made this rule one of his top ten: "You shall not lie." It's the ninth commandment. It's always best to tell the truth. Let's make God happy and tell the truth. Then we'll really be winners!**

TOUR GUIDE TIP You may want to have small prizes on hand to give to the kids for playing the game. Give them pieces of candy, small toys, or stickers. Let the kids share about times they were deceived, and encourage them to share how they felt about it.

STORY EXCURSION (15 minutes)
Lila's Web of Lies

Items to Pack: crepe paper streamers

"Oh what a tangled web we weave, when first we practice to deceive!" In this activity, children will experience the truth of this quote from Sir Walter Scott. Seat the kids on chairs in a circle. Tell the children that as you tell this story, you will wind crepe paper around them each time a lie is told in the story. As you wrap the crepe paper around the children, go in and out of the circle, around children, and across the circle to create a very tangled mess.

Say: "Bethany got promoted into third grade!"

Lila's mouth dropped open when she heard the news. "But I'm a better reader than Bethany," thought Lila. Bethany stumbled over a lot of words. But Lila flew through every page. "I'm smarter than Bethany," thought Lila. "I'm the one who should have been promoted." Lila slumped down in her chair and pouted all afternoon.

When Lila's mom asked her how school went, Lila got a sly grin on her face. "It went great," she said. "In fact, I'm doing so great that Mrs. Miller is putting me ahead into third grade!" Lila didn't know she was going to say that. The lie just sort of popped out, and when it did, it sounded pretty good.

"Wow! That's great, honey," Lila's mom said. "Congratulations." Mom phoned Grandma with the good news. Lila's older sister and brother slapped her on the back and high-fived her. Dad brought her a fancy pen home from the office. Lila tried to forget God's commandment "You shall not lie." Still, she knew that ⏾ it's always best to tell the truth.

After two days, Lila's mom said, "I'm surprised your teacher hasn't called me yet to talk about your school situation."

"Oh, she will," Lila said. "She's sending home some papers soon." Lila couldn't believe how quickly that new lie slipped out of her mouth.

Two days later a special package arrived from Grandma and Grandpa. It was an A++ doll that had its own backpack, little textbooks, and a report card to fill out. Lila thought, "Whoa, they're really believing this." She called her grandparents and told them third grade was easy so far. Ouch! Lying to Grandma and Grandpa hurt.

Before Lila left for school the next morning, her mom handed her a note. Lila promised to give it to her teacher. It read, "Dear Mrs. Miller: Will Lila need any special supplies for third grade? Who is her new teacher? Do I need to come in for a conference?" Lila stuffed the note into her backpack. At school, she ripped it up in the bathroom and threw it away. When Lila got home, her mom handed her a congratulation card from her uncle. It had five dollars inside. Lila's smile drooped. Her uncle was a pastor. Lila had to write him a thank-you card, telling him she liked third grade. That night Lila prayed, "Dear God, I know ⏾ it's always best to tell the truth, but if you'll let me get away with this one lie, I promise I'll never lie again."

"I wonder why your teacher hasn't answered my note yet?" Mom asked.

Lila thought fast. "Uh...she couldn't read the note. She was crying so hard because she misses me so much."

Mom's eyes narrowed, and she stared hard at Lila. Lila tried to make her big, brown eyes look even bigger. Her mother said, "You know, ⏾ it's always best to tell the truth."

When Jamie came to play, Mom said, "Jamie, I'll bet you miss Lila being in your class."

"Why would I?" Jamie asked and skipped away.

Lila's mom put her hands on her hips, and Lila whispered to her mother, "Jamie's just jealous because she wasn't put ahead into third grade too."

That night Lila thought, "This isn't so great anymore. But I can't get out of these lies now." Lila dreamed she had a spider body and her own head. She was caught in a big, sticky web and couldn't get out. Lila woke up sweating. "This definitely isn't fun anymore," Lila said out loud. Luckily, her sister was asleep.

The next day was Lila's birthday party. The girls loved Lila's A++ doll. At the party, Dad said, "Let's congratulate Lila for being promoted to third grade."

"For what?" Tiffany asked.

"Lila didn't get promoted," said Krista. "She still sits right by me."

Lila tried to kick Krista under the table but missed.

Lila's mom and dad took her into the den. Lila told them the truth. "I'm sorry. It's just that one lie led to the next and the next, and then it was like this big web I couldn't get out of and—and—and..." Lila started crying. The birthday party was ruined. Lila had to send the doll and money back with apology notes. Lila's friends told the kids at school about Lila's big lie. "No wonder God commanded us not to lie," thought Lila. "Now I can see that 🌑 it's always best to tell the truth!"

Have the kids try to get untangled from the crepe paper. When they have freed themselves, ask:

• How did you feel all wrapped up in the crepe paper?

• How is this mess like what happened when Lila lied?

• Why does God command us not to lie?

Say: God told us, "You shall not lie," because he doesn't want us to get into a messy web of lies. He loves us too much to see us hurt others and ourselves. 🌑 It's always best to tell the truth, even when you'd be embarrassed by the truth or you're afraid the truth will bring a punishment. If you find yourself telling one lie, tell the truth right away so you don't get caught in a messy web of lies as Lila did!

<table>
<tr><td>ADVENTURE
IN LIVING
GOD'S
LAWS</td><td></td></tr>
</table>

(10 minutes)
Lies and God's Eyes

In this activity, the children will make writing appear with water and crayons to show that even when we try to cover up our lies, God sees through it all.

Preparation: Mix a drop of blue food coloring and the cup of water in the resealable plastic bag.

Items to Pack: strong resealable plastic bag, 1 cup of water, blue food coloring, piece of white paper, blue crayon, orange crayon

Say: Mandy had a problem. She had borrowed her sister's china animals for Show and Tell without asking anyone. On the way home, Mandy dropped the bag of animals. Every miniature animal was shattered. Mandy swept all the broken pieces back into the bag and hid it under her bed before her sister got home. When her mom asked her what she used for Show and Tell, Mandy told her mom that she showed the class her seashells.

Ask:

• What did Mandy say that she brought to class?

Write "seashells" in orange on the paper. Have each child scribble over the word "seashells" with the blue crayon. Tell children that the blue marks they make are like the lies Mandy told to cover up what she had done. While each child is scribbling, ask him or her why Mandy lied.

After each child has had a turn, say: Mandy took her sister's animals and broke them. Then she lied to cover up her mistake. We often lie to hide another sin, just as the word "seashells" is hiding under the marks you made. But God has very special eyes. He can see right through our lies.

Take the bag of blue water, and lay it over the paper. Let the kids see the words pop out. Read Genesis 18:15 and ask:

• Why did Sarah lie?

• How is that like Mandy's problem?

<table>
<tr><td>TOUR
GUIDE
TIP</td><td></td></tr>
</table>

If you have more than ten children in your class, form two groups, and have each group do this activity separately.

• How are the marks we made with blue crayons like Mandy's lie?

• What can you do if you are afraid to tell the truth?

Say: Mandy lied about the animals because she was afraid of the consequences from breaking them. "Consequences" means what happens to you for doing something. Mandy will have to suffer the consequences of breaking the animals and now also for lying. If you lie, you need to be truthful as soon as possible. God can see through all our lies anyway! Most people will be happy to forgive you. It's always best to tell the truth.

Items to Pack: for each child, 1 large sheet of newsprint, scissors, markers

(25 minutes)
Take Off the Old Self

In this activity, children will make full body sketches to use as they talk about our old and new selves.

Say: When you decide to follow Christ, the Bible says you become a brand-new person (2 Corinthians 5:17). You may still tell a lie every now and then, but you'll be sorry about it and try to obey God's commandments. Read Colossians 3:9-10a: "Do not lie to each other, since you have taken off your old self with its practices and have put on the new self." Let's make an old self that was used to lying and a new self that realizes that it's always best to tell the truth.

Assign partners. Double the newsprint into two layers. Have the kids take turns lying down on the newsprint and having their partners trace around them. Then have the each child cut out two body shapes from the double layer of newsprint. Have them label one the "Old Self" and the other the "New Self." On the Old Self have them write, "I'm sorry for lying about..." and write in times they've lied. On the New Self, they can write, "It's always best to tell the truth," the verse from Colossians, and the ninth commandment. Have the younger kids color the New Self with bright colors and the Old Self with dark colors. Keep these to use for the closing prayer.

SCENIC ROUTE ➡
Reiterate the fact to your children that lies almost always cover up another sin. Have the kids cover up their lies on the Old Self with sticky tabs. Have them write on the sticky tabs, "Lies try to hide my sins. I can't lie to God. He sees within."

Items to Pack: crayons, tape or glue, and, for each child, 1 photocopy of the "Let the Truth Pop Out" handout (p. 97), scissors

SOUVENIRS ➡ (15 minutes)
Let the Truth Pop Out

Make a sample card while the children watch. Then have the children make their own while you ask the following questions. Younger children may need help folding the lips. When the children have finished their work, they can decorate the front of the card. Have the children say the poem aloud together while making the mouth move. Have each child get together with a partner and exchange cards. Ask kids to sign the back of the other person's card as a commitment to tell the truth and return the card.

Ask:

• Why is it always best to tell the truth?

• How can you let your lips speak the truth?

• Why does God say, "You shall not lie"?

• What are some lies that are easy for you to slip into?

Say: It can be tough to always tell the truth. God called you to be his special people. God's special people tell the truth. Let your lips flap only the truth!

 (15 minutes)
One Little Lie

Preparation: Try this at home first so you know how it works.

Items to Pack: one 8-ounce clear glass, water, food coloring, cup of bleach

Fill the glass one-third full with water. Gather the children around a table where they can see what you are doing. Say: **Let's pretend that this clear water is a newborn baby. Babies have not yet sinned; they are innocent. But babies grow up.**

Now let's pretend the water is the baby who is now an older child. Pour in a little more water. **This boy takes his brother's toy race car and breaks it. He hides the pieces. When his brother asks him where the race car is, he lies.** Pour a tiny drop of food coloring into the water. Stir it. Let the kids watch it swirl around. **One little lie and this innocent child became a liar.** Have a child read Revelation 21:8: "The cowardly, the unbelieving, the vile, the murderers…and all liars—their place will be in the fiery lake of burning sulfur."

Ask:

• **What will happen to liars?**

• **Does that seem fair to you? Why or why not?**

Say: **That's the bad news. Luckily for us, God didn't leave us in this awful situation. In Isaiah 53 we hear that Jesus poured out his life for us.** Pour the bleach into the water. **Jesus Christ took the punishment for our lies so that we could be clean, innocent, and pure, like this water.** Hold it up to the light for the kids to see. **What would we do without Jesus? We'd be caught by our own lies. When you ask Jesus to forgive you and give your life to him, he'll make you completely clean!**

TOUR GUIDE TIP Teachers, please be careful that none of the bleach splashes into the children's eyes or on their hands. Set it up before class, and after the activity immediately put all materials out of reach to keep kids away from it.

TRAVEL-ALONG COMMANDMENT SONG (5 minutes)

Teach your kids these lines and motions. See pages 6-8 to review the song up to this point.

I see ten fingers, you shall not lie. *(Hold up ten fingers.)*

You're number nine; you gotta try *(fold the thumb on one hand into the palm)*

To tell the truth, it's always best. *(Make fists and raise them overhead.)*

God commanded, he didn't suggest. *(Point finger.)*

 (5 minutes)

Say: **While I pray this verse from Colossians 3:9, take the body shape you made labeled Old Self, the one that was used to telling lies, wad it up, and throw it away. This will show God that you know it's best to tell the truth. Keep your New Self, and hang it in your room to remind you of how Jesus gives us new life.**

Dear Lord, we want to obey you when you say, "Do not lie to each other, since you have taken off your old self with its practices." We put on our new selves. We know it's always best to tell the truth. Thank you for helping us tell the truth, and forgive us when we slip up and tell lies. Amen.

Items to Pack: Old and New Selves made from newsprint in the "Take Off the Old Self" activity

Items to Pack: copying machine, dark markers, paper; optional, colored paper or paper with pre-printed borders

(10 minutes)
Coming Into the Light With Photocopies

Recording our thoughts and ideas today includes the use of technology. Photocopying using light-sensitive paper was introduced in the early and mid-1800s. Early images were developed on photographic paper to make copies. Let your kids experience seeing a commandment altered on a copy machine.

1. Have kids write out the commandment in dark letters.

2. When they photocopy their papers, let the children experiment by adding their own handprint and trinkets or stickers around the commandment to decorate it.

3. Show the kids how you can enlarge, reduce, lighten, or darken their images.

4. As an option, use paper with pre-printed borders or a variety of colors.

Extra Cool

Make a negative image using special paper at a hobby store. Ask for paper that allows you to make sun prints. This paper allows you to lay an object on it, expose it to sun, and produce an image. You need a sunny day and letters cut out of foam to make the commandment with this method.

Did You Know?

Did you know that the Greek word "photo" means "light" and the Greek word "graphia" means "writing"? So photography is really writing with light. The method used in copy machines today—electrostatic photocopying—was invented in America by Chester Carlson in 1938. His process is completely dry. The word "xeros" means "dry," and the word xerography is the name for making copies with this method.

Did You Know?

Did you know that copy machines use static electricity to hold the powdered ink onto the surface of the paper? It's a little like a balloon sticking to a wall after you rub it on your hair. Then heat melts the ink (or toner) to create a permanent image. Isn't it incredible that all of that can happen in just a few seconds?

Let the Truth Pop Out

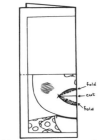

Fold in half lengthwise and cut horizontal slit in the mouth.

Open and fold in quarters with mouth on inside.

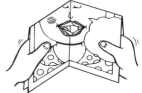

Push lips out from center fold.

"You shall not lie,"

God says…

Tell the truth.

So I'm going to always try to

JOURNEY 11

The Tenth Commandment: You Shall Not Want What Others Have

Pathway Point: 🌐 Be happy with what you have.

In-Focus Verse: "You shall not covet your neighbor's house. You shall not covet your neighbor's wife, or his manservant or maidservant, his ox or donkey, or anything that belongs to your neighbor" (Exodus 20:17).

Travel Itinerary

The desire to acquire is a national epidemic. When 93 percent of teenage girls choose shopping as their favorite pastime, you know commercialism is consuming us. Advertisers target our children. Commercial after commercial convinces our kids that they *must* have something they had never heard of until a minute ago. Outstretched fingers and whining cries become the dominant voices in our homes. While God's other laws focus on what we do, this commandment hits us where it hurts—our secret cravings.

The Apostle Paul said, "I have learned to be content." The Hebrew word for contentment, "arkeo," means "to be strong, to defend, to ward off." Contentment, then, is not a passive state; it's a muscle that needs exercise. Contentment liberates a greedy heart and reins in a wandering one. This lesson gives your kids a cure for the gimmes. It's designed to teach children to be aware of greed, defuse it, and defeat it with thankfulness. To counter covetousness and count our blessings, we need to come back full circle to the first commandment: "Give God first place in your heart."

DEPARTURE PRAYER (5 minutes)

When you pray with the children, pull up an empty chair. When they ask you what it's for, read to them Matthew 18:20: "For where two or three come together in my name, there am I with them." Tell them you've invited Jesus.

Dear Lord Jesus, we are here together in your name. Lord, we already have so many things, but we want so many more. Help us to be happy with what we have. Teach us to be thankful for everything you've given us. Help us to sharpen our eyes when the greedies come. Help us to strengthen our thankfulness muscles. Help us to give you first place in our hearts. Amen.

1st STOP DISCOVERY (20 minutes) Gettin' the Greedies

This version of "Dirty Santa" will expose covetousness in even the youngest child.

Preparation: On the small pieces of paper, number from one to the total number of students you have. Place each candy bar in a bag, and put the bags on a table.

Let each child draw a number. The child who draws the number one chooses a bag, opens it, and pulls out the candy bar. The child who draws the number two may either select a new bag or take the first child's candy bar. If he or she chooses number one's candy, then the child who drew the number one can pick a new bag. The child who draws the number three gets the same choices, and so on. Each child *must* give up his or her candy if someone asks for it. When every child has a candy bar, the game is over.

Ask:

• **How did you feel when you saw a candy bar you wanted?**

• **What do you wish you could have done to get it?**

Say: All of us sometimes want things that belong to someone else. This is called coveting. That greedy feeling of wanting what others have breaks God's tenth commandment: "You shall not want what others have." The Bible teaches us to be happy with what we have. Let's munch on these candy bars with a happy heart, focusing on our own yummy candy bars and not our neighbors'.

Items to Pack: for each child, 1 of a variety of candy bars, paper lunch bag, small piece of paper

STORY EXCURSION (10 minutes)
Helen Has to Have Her Horses

In this activity, children will help tell Helen's story.

You can include all of the children in this story. Write the poem on the board, and go over it once or twice. Tell the kids that they should recite the poem each time you put on the Helen mask.

Say: **Helen loved horses. She loved to touch their silky manes and nuzzle their muzzles. She wore her hair in ponytails. Helen's whole bedroom looked like a stable. Helen even had a bedspread with horses all over it. But the first thing you'd notice in Helen's room was her model horse collection. The shelves were filled with model horses: Appaloosas, Clydesdales, Arabians, and more.**

For every birthday and Christmas for the last three years, Helen had asked for and received new model horses. In fact, in her collection she had every model horse except one. It was a miniature Shetland pony. The stores had been sold out of it for months. But that didn't stop Helen from wanting it. She wasn't ⬥ happy with what she had; Helen had to have that Shetland pony.

Items to Pack: enlarged picture of Helen from the "What's Inside You?" handout (p. 106), cut and pasted onto cardboard to form a mask

Put on the Helen mask, and encourage the children to say the poem.

Now Helen was usually pretty sweet,

But when she wanted something, she wasn't too neat.

"I want it. I need it. I gotta have it," she'd say.

She'd throw a fit if she didn't get her way.

"I want what I want, and I want it now.

I'll get what I want, and I don't care how!"

"Drive to Mintona, and get me that Shetland pony," Helen told her mom. **"I heard it's in Karen's Collectible Store."**

Her mom replied, **"Helen, Mintona is three hours away, and that pony costs**

TOUR GUIDE TIP When you tell this story, be sure to use changes of tone in your voice. For the poem, use your ugliest, greediest voice. The children's ears will perk up, and you'll get their attention. If you have a child named Helen in your class, you may want to change the character's name.

more than fifteen of your other model horses put together."

Put on the Helen mask, and recite the poem with the kids.

Helen sulked and pouted. Her mother said, "Helen, why can't you learn to 🌑 be happy with what you have?" But Helen didn't hear her. She had dumped her piggy bank and was counting her money again.

Helen had a very best friend named Jamie. Jamie liked horses, but not as much as Helen did. Jamie only had a horse calendar hanging in her room.

One day Jamie and her mom were at a yard sale. Jamie was digging through a box of small toys when she spotted a horse's hoof. What did that hoof belong to? Jamie pulled it out. It was the Shetland pony model! Jamie dug in her pocket for her money. "Will you take fifty cents for this?" she asked.

"Sure," the lady said. Jamie took the pony home and put it on her dresser.

The next day, Helen went over to play. When she went into Jamie's room, she stopped in her tracks. Her eyes widened.

"You...you...you have it!" Helen said, heading for the pony.

"Oh, yeah," Jamie said, flopping down on her bed. "I got that yesterday."

Put on the mask, and recite the poem. Encourage the children to say the poem with you.

Helen picked up the pony and stroked its mane. "You must have paid a fortune for it," Helen whispered.

"Nope. I got it for fifty cents at a yard..."

"Fifty cents! *You* got *my* pony for *fifty* cents?"

Jamie grabbed the pony out of Helen's hands. "It's not *your* pony; it's mine."

Helen grabbed it back. "You know I've been wanting this Shetland for six months! It's not fair!" Then Helen's voice got a little softer. Trying her sweetest, drippiest voice, she said, "Jamie, we've been best friends for a long time, and I always take you horseback riding and..."

"I thought you wanted a friend to ride with," Jamie said, quite hurt.

Put on the mask, and recite the poem. Encourage the children to say the poem with you.

Helen threw the pony on Jamie's bed and stormed out of the house. She went home and sat in her room, pouting and feeling very sorry for herself.

Helen looked up at her shelves. The Palomino's big brown eyes stared back at her. Helen sighed. Then she looked at her poster of the Ten Commandments. The tenth commandment seemed to leap out at her: "You shall not want what others have." Helen prayed to God, "I'm sorry. I know I've broken your commandment, and I've coveted Jamie's pony. Help me to 🌑 be happy with what I have." One by one, Helen went through all her horses and thanked God for each horse and each person who gave it to her. Then she picked out three horses and put them in a box. She took the box to Jamie's house.

"Here, Jamie," Helen said.

Jamie opened the box. A big grin spread over her face. "Thanks!" she said.

"No," Helen said, "Thank *you*. Thank you for teaching me to 🌑 be happy with what I have. It's the only way to live."

Jamie said, "Now my pony won't be lonely." The friends giggled together.

Ask:

• How did Helen feel about Jamie's pony?

• Can you share a time you felt like that?

• How can you learn to be happy with what you have?

Say: Helen felt as though she had to have that pony. That's coveting. God tells us in his tenth commandment, "You shall not want what others have." Sometimes it's hard to tell your heart how to feel. But if you thank God for what he has given you, you'll learn to ⬩ be happy with what you have.

Green With Greed

ADVENTURE IN LIVING GOD'S LAWS

(15 minutes)

This funny skit shows the kids how thankfulness cures greediness.

Preparation: Choose two kids to read this skit. Have one child make green marks on his or her face.

Items to Pack: 2 copies of the "Green With Greed" script (p. 105); green washable marker; 2 baby wipes; jar of jelly beans labeled, "Thank-Pill-Ness: This cures covetousness"; extra jelly beans for class; optional extras, lab coat, stethoscope

Ask:

• What was Greenie's real problem?

• How is Greenie like you sometimes?

• How can you cure your greedies?

Have the children form pairs and take turns. One child will thank God for his or her blessings while the other will dole out a jellybean with each prayer of thanks.

Setting Your Heart on Things Above

(15 minutes)

Children will get the opportunity to experience thankfulness in this simple activity.

Items to Pack: for each child, 2 index cards, scissors, 1 sheet of red construction paper, pen

Have each child cut out a large heart and write his or her name on it.

Ask:

• What are some things that kids today want?

Record their answers individually on index cards. Place the index cards around on the floor. Have the kids go around the room with their hearts. If a child has ever wanted something on one of the cards, he or she should place his or her heart on it. Have a child read Colossians 3:1-2.

Ask:

• What are some "things above" that we should set our hearts on?

Record those answers on index cards as well. If the kids get stuck for answers, have them look up these verses or related ones: Psalm 105:4; Colossians 3:12; and Hebrews 10:23. Place these answers up high on a wall. The children can go around again, this time setting each heart on one of the "things above" listed on the cards. Afterward, have children write on their hearts, "Set your hearts on things above" (Colossians 3:1). Then they can take their hearts home.

Ask:

• How does "setting your heart on things above" help you keep God's commandment to not want what others have?

• Which of the things above do you need to set your heart on?

• How can you do that?

Say: The secret to not wanting what others have is  being happy with what you do have. Learn to count "things above" as some of your most prized possessions. After all, they are the only things that will last!

SOUVENIRS → (20 minutes)
Has-to-Have-It Helen

In this activity, children will cut and paste items they want and write down items they are thankful for.

Preparation: Have the blank paper already divided and labeled for the younger children.

Have each child create a self-portrait on the right side of the handout by coloring in his or her own skin tones, hair color, clothes, and so on. Have children write their names at the tops, and girls should add an "s" in the blank to make "she." Have children cut on the dotted line and set that paper aside. On the blank paper, have the kids draw a vertical line to divide the paper in half lengthwise. Have them write on the bottom left side, "You shall not want what others have." On the bottom right side, have the children write, "Be happy with what you have."

Have the children go through the toy and clothing pictures and cut out what they might like to have, gluing those pictures on the left side of the page. On the right side, have them write specific people or things they have and are thankful for. For example, they might write, "my house," "my friend Katie," and "my new cleats." Staple each child's portrait page on top of his or her "What's Inside You?" page.

Ask:

• What are some of the things Helen has to have?

• How could this break the tenth commandment?

• How can you avoid becoming like "Has-to-Have-It Helen"?

Say: The more stuff Helen had, the unhappier she became. We break the tenth commandment when we stop just *liking* what a person has and start thinking, "I *have* to have that!" This comes close to breaking the first and second commandments, too. Do you remember what they are?

TRAVEL-ALONG COMMANDMENT SONG (5 minutes)

Teach your kids these lines and motions. See pages 6-8 to review up to this point.

Put up ten fingers. Pull 'em in, in, in. (*Hold up ten fingers, then close both hands into fists.*)

To want, want, want, can be a sin. (*Hold up ten fingers, then make fists.*)

You shall not want what others have got. (*Reach out with hands and then pull in as if grabbing something.*)

Be happy, 'cause you've got a lot. (*Make a circle with both hands in front of body.*)

ONE WAY ▶ (5 minutes)
Drawing the Line Between Right and Wrong

In this activity, children will cross the line from admiration to sin.

Items to Pack: masking tape, pen for each child

Lay a long piece of masking tape on the floor. Have some of the children write, "You shall not want what others have," on the tape. Have all the children stand on one side of the line.

Say: **The law says, "You shall not covet or want what others have." That's a lot to ask. Name one thing that a friend of yours has that you don't have. Now if you have ever wished that thing were yours, step over the line.** After the kids have all done so, say: **You have all coveted; so have I. That makes us lawbreakers. God says that no lawbreakers will enter heaven.** (See Ephesians 5:5.) **But he didn't leave us hopeless! He sent his Son, Jesus, to die on the cross.** (Add another piece of masking tape to the one already on the floor to form a cross.) **God forgives us for being lawbreakers when we trust Jesus to forgive our sins.**

HOME AGAIN PRAYER (5 minutes)

Have the children form a circle, holding their "What's Inside You?" handouts. Have them go around the circle, thanking God for the things they have written on the left side. Teach them to pray by having them say, "Thank you, God, for [name of thing]." You can close with the following prayer:

Dear Lord, you have given us so much. Besides all the wonderful things we have at home, we have a God who loves us and smiles on us. We have you, Jesus, as our best friend, and we have a home in heaven waiting for us. You are so kind! Help us to be happy with what we have. We want to obey you when you tell us that we should not want what others have. We're so glad we have you! Amen.

TOUR GUIDE TIP

Often, children who are new to praying are uncomfortable with talking directly to God. They will try a less personal "I'm thankful for..." Teach them the more proactive way of saying "Thank you, God, for..." Over time, with love, practice, and patience, you will have the extraordinary privilege of hearing true prayers pour forth from a true heart. Keep up the great job!

(15 minutes)

Items to Pack: computer with a color printer

Computerrific!

Computer technology changes our world at a dizzying rate, and it has greatly changed the way we record our thoughts and ideas. What was imagined last year becomes archaic next year. Let your kids have fun with their last commandment by typing into the computer themselves and decorating their pages with clip art, borders, fancy print, and more. If you aren't familiar with computer graphics, find someone at your church who is, or ask the youth to help you.

1. Type the tenth commandment into the computer.

2. Experiment with different type fonts, colors, and sizes. Center the commandment and add clip art.

3. Add borders.

You may want to use a decorative paper. Make a sample, copy it, and let the kids color it while they are waiting to make their own.

Extra Cool

You can buy special programs that manipulate images by changing the pictures and words, stretching them, spinning them, and reversing them. The Internet is a great source of free graphics to add to your commandment page.

Did You Know?

Did you know that computers can see for blind people and talk to them? The blind person scans in a page, and the computer reads it out loud. Some computers can tell who you are by your voice patterns and how your voice rises and falls. Then the computer can talk back to you. Each new computer model becomes more and more human.

Did You Know?

Did you know that the first computers took up the space of about four bedrooms? Now some computer chips are smaller than your fingernails! Computers can be found everywhere: in spacecraft circling planets; under the sea, probing the ocean floor; in our homes; in cars; and in kids' toys. How many computers do you use every day without being aware of them?

Green With Greed

Greenie: (*Crying*) Doctor, doctor, *help*! I've got a case of the greenies.

Doctor: Let's check the symptoms. Hmmm, has your neighbor gotten something new?

Greenie: Well, now that you mention it, my neighbor does have a new four-wheeler. Oh, that motor hums, and you ought to see the crazy colors it's painted, and it goes, like, fifty miles an hour, and...

Doctor: Yes, I see. And have you been wishing you had one like it?

Greenie: You bet I have! I've wanted one just like it since that first zroom...

Doctor: I see. And have you been dreaming of ways to get one yourself?

Greenie: Boy, have I! I've been looking in the paper for one and saving my money for one and...

Doctor: Aha! My friend, what you have is not so much a case of the greenies. You have a bad case of the *greedies*!

Greenie: Oh, no! Doctor, what can I do?

Doctor: (*Handing Greenie the jar*) This jar of Thank-Pill-Ness will cure most covetousness, greediness, and downright wanting what others have.

Greenie: How often do I take them?

Doctor: Any time you feel the greedies coming on, thank God for what you do have. You will overcome the greedies by being happy with what you have.

Greenie: OK, doc.

Greenie thanks God for things and people and all the blessings of God in his life. Each time he does, he pops a jelly bean into his mouth and uses the baby wipe to wipe off a spot of green marker until the spots and jelly beans are gone.

What's Inside You?

_____ is happy with what ___he has!

Helen has to have it!

JOURNEY 12

Reviewing the Top Ten

Pathway Point: God's treasured people choose to obey.

In-Focus verse: "Now if you obey me fully and keep my covenant, then out of all nations you will be my treasured possession. Although the whole earth is mine, you will be for me a kingdom of priests and a holy nation" (Exodus 19:5-6a).

Travel Itinerary

When God repeats his law in Deuteronomy, I see our Sovereign Lord down on his knees, begging Israel to follow him. I feel God's heart beating, see his arms outstretched, and hear his cries: "Love me, obey me, cling to me!" God even provided blessings for obedience and deadly curses for disobedience. Some would say it was rather a "no-brainer" proposition. Did Israel choose obedience and life? No. Do we?

Just as the children of Israel had completed their desert trek and were being launched into their new land, your children are wrapping up their journeys through God's loving laws. When they leave your classroom, they will be faced with many opportunities to obey or disobey God's laws. This lesson emphasizes that they have a choice to live as God's treasured possessions if they obey. Since none of us can obey fully, be sure to do the last activity to show them that, ultimately, it's not our obedience, but our faith in Jesus Christ that gives us the hope of life.

TOUR GUIDE TIP

Out of all the lessons in this book, please be sure to do the "One-Way Sign" activity in this lesson. Today's point is that God's treasured people choose to obey. We don't want to let the kids leave class, disobey, and feel they are out of God's family. Make sure you tell them clearly that they need to decide to obey and try to obey, but being in God's family is a matter of faith in Christ. See John 1:12.

DEPARTURE PRAYER (10 minutes)

Show the children that a relationship with God includes talking to God through prayer. Say the lines with the children. Open your Bible, and show them God's reply in Scripture. Personalize it.

Children: Dear Lord, thank you for your commandments. Please help us to obey.

God's reply in the Bible: Children, let my commandments become a part of your heart. Talk about them when you sit at home and when you walk along the road, when you lie down and when you get up (Deuteronomy 6:6-9).

Children: Thank you for choosing us to be your treasured people who choose to obey you.

God's reply in the Bible: I didn't pick you because you are smart or strong. I chose you because I love you (Deuteronomy 7:7-8).

Children: We love you, too. Help us to love and obey your Laws. Amen.

Items to Pack: party items, such as cake, balloons, horn blowers, streamers, confetti; and, for each child, paper, pencils

STOP 1st DISCOVERY (25 minutes)
A No-Brainer

In this activity, children will choose between having a party and doing nothing.

Preparation: Set up the party on one side of the room. On the other side, leave a defined area with only a few chairs. The idea is to make one side attractive and the other side sparse. As the kids come in, have them sit in the middle, between the party (blessings) side and the sparse (curses) side.

Say: You have a choice today of which side you choose to be on—the blessings side or the curses side. To be on the blessings side, you have to obey me. You have to go over to the table and write out all the commandments. If you choose to disobey me, you can go to the other side of the room and sit quietly on a chair. The choice is yours.

Let the kids decide. Use this time as a review of the commandments. You may want to pass around some photocopies of the commandments (page 10) to help the kids who can't remember all of them. The older kids can help the younger ones. When all have finished, you can have an obedience party and celebrate with cake and confetti.

While kids are eating, ask:

• Why did you choose to be on the blessings side?

• What did you have to do to be part of the obedience party?

Say: God lets us choose whether we will obey his commandments or not. If we do, he heaps tons of blessings on us. We become his precious treasure, his celebration! If we won't obey, bad things can come our way. The people of Israel were also given the choice of blessings for obeying God's commandments or curses for disobeying. Listen to their choices. Read aloud Deuteronomy 11:26-28, 28:1-13, and 28:15-20.

Ask:

• What choices did the Israelites have?

• What do you think they chose to do?

• What would you have chosen if you were an Israelite?

• What do you choose today?

Say: God gave the Israelites an easy decision, a "no-brainer." Let's see from the story if ◑ God's treasured people chose to obey him.

TOUR GUIDE TIP Copy the commandments (p. 10), but cover some of the words for the little ones to fill in. For example, for "You shall not lie," cover the word "lie," and ask the children what word belongs in the blank. For the older kids, cover up all the words, leaving only the shape of the tablets.

STORY EXCURSION (20 minutes)
God's People Disobey (Exodus 24, 32, and 34)

Preparation: Choose someone to act as Moses during the story. Have a partition set up with someone ready to hand the commandments to "Moses."

Say: Remember when God gave Moses the Ten Commandments? Thunder crashed and lightening flashed to show how serious God is about his laws. The people responded with one voice: "Everything the Lord has said we will do." *(Have the children repeat: "Everything the Lord has said we will do.")* They ◑ chose to obey because they wanted to be God's treasured people. They didn't how hard it would be.

God asked Moses to build an altar (a pile of rocks) and to burn an animal on it.

Items to Pack: toy cow, music, player for music, 2 sets of foam tablets with the Ten Commandments written on them, pitcher of water, yellow or orange flavored drink powder, and, for each child, stone, cup, paper towel

(Have all the kids put their stones in a pile.) Now this may sound strange to you, but God wanted the people to understand one very important thing: It is the blood that makes up for our sins (Leviticus 17:11). *(Have the kids repeat: "It is the blood that makes up for our sins.")* Even though 🌑 God's treasured people choose to obey, there will be times when we don't. So God, in his kindness, allows something else to pay the price for our sins.

Moses climbed back up the mountain, and God gave Moses two tablets of stone, inscribed by the finger of God. God's very own hand wrote out his ten loving laws. *(Have the person behind the partition give Moses the commandments.)*

While Moses was with God, the Israelites, God's chosen, handpicked, special, treasured people chose to disobey. They said, "We don't know what has happened to Moses." *(Have the kids repeat: "We don't know what has happened to Moses.")* They told Aaron, Moses' brother, to make them an idol, or a fake god. And Aaron did it! He actually had them throw all their gold, even their earrings, into the fire. He shaped the gold into a calf, or a baby cow. The people gave a party for their little cow idol. They said, "This is your god, O Israel, who brought you up out of Egypt." *(Turn on some music, and have the kids circle around the toy cow.)*

Just then, Moses came down from the mountain. He saw the people dancing and laughing around their idol. Moses' anger burned. He raised those stone tablets over his head and threw them down, smashing them to pieces. *(Moses smashes the commandments.)* The music stopped. *(Stop the music.)* The people stood there, caught. Uh-oh. They knew they were in big trouble.

Moses didn't say a word. He just took that calf and threw it in the fire. They watched it melt—first the tail, then the hind legs, then the rest of it. Then Moses took that melted gold and began pounding it, and pounding it, and pounding it until it was as thin as powder. Then he took that gold powder and scattered it in the water. *(Moses sprinkles flavored drink powder into the water.)*

"Drink it," he yelled. *(Pour the drink into the kids' cups, and have them drink it.)*

As the people swallowed their fake little god, they saw how foolish they had been. God was tired of their sin. He was ready to destroy them. Moses said, "Whoever is for the Lord, come to me." *(Have the kids go to Moses.)* God's treasured people must choose to obey, no matter how hard it is. Moses knew that he had to stop the people's sin before God destroyed all of them.

With a sigh, Moses climbed back up the mountain. He carried two new blank stone tablets. *(Moses lays the tablets down.)* He stayed on that mountain for forty more days and forty more nights without eating any food or drinking any water. What was he doing that whole time? Moses was lying on the cold, jagged rocks, with his face down. Was he taking a nap? No. He was begging God to spare the people. (See Deuteronomy 9:18; 10:10-11, 25-26.) *(Have Moses lie down and plead for the people. Have the person behind the partition flip over the tablets.)*

When Moses got up, what did he see? God's loving laws, written once more by the finger of God. He hugged those two tablets to his chest. Moses knew that God was giving the Israelites a second chance. And that's the kind of God we have, a God who always gives us a second and a third, fourth, fifth *(have the kids hold up two fingers, then three, and so on)*, and ninetieth chance, if only we ask for forgiveness. This time when

SCENIC ROUTE → You can make this story unforgettable by making Moses' face really glow! Have him put some white face paint on his face, and use a black light. Make sure Moses isn't wearing white clothes because the white clothes will compete for attention with his face. If you don't have a black light, it would be worthwhile to purchase one. You'll use this investment many times. Read 2 Corinthians 3:7-18 to the older kids, and explain further about the New Covenant. Have them create veils of their own from pieces of cloth, and write the verse from 2 Corinthians 3:16 on their veils.

Moses came down the mountain, he didn't hear any music, but the people all shrank back from him in fear. Why? Because this time Moses' face was glowing. It was shining so brightly that he actually had to put a veil over his face. *(Have the kids put paper towels over their faces.)* The Law is like the veil; it is between God and man. But when Jesus forgives us, the veil is taken away. *(Have the kids take their towels off.)*

Ask:

• How did God's treasured people disobey?

• Why did God not destroy them?

• How does God forgive us today?

Say: God didn't destroy all of his treasured people, not even when they made an idol, because Moses begged for forgiveness. Today, Jesus' blood forgives us.

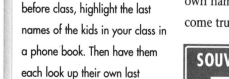

ADVENTURE IN LIVING GOD'S LAWS (15 minutes)
God's Dream Come True

In this activity, children will find their names hidden among many to know how special they are to God.

Preparation: Cut the paper into strips. Write each child's name on a separate slip of paper. On extra slips, write other first names.

Ask:

• What is your big dream in life?

• Did you know God has a dream too?

Draw two closed eyes and a smile on the poster board. Draw a big thought balloon coming from the smiling face. On the bottom, write, "God's Dream."

Say and write on the top: **You are God's dream come true, his treasure.**

Ask:

• As God's special treasures, how should you behave?

Scatter the slips of paper on the floor around the room. Tell children to find their own names and tape them into God's dream balloon to show that they are God's dream come true, his special treasure. (You'll use this at the end of the lesson as well.)

SOUVENIRS (15 minutes)
Rights and Responsibilities of the Crown

In this activity, the children will make crowns and decorate them.

Preparation: Make a crown for yourself first.

Have kids cut out the crown along the bold lines. Display the crown you made. While kids work, ask:

• Can you name a queen, king, prince, or princess?

• What is his or her job?

• How are you like a prince or princess in God's eyes?

• What are your jobs as children of the King?

Items to Pack: poster board, marker, masking tape, paper, scissors

SCENIC ROUTE To make this activity more personal, take pictures of the kids with an instant-print camera, and hang the pictures under their names. Also, before class, highlight the last names of the kids in your class in a phone book. Then have them each look up their own last names, emphasizing how God seeks them out.

Items to Pack: tape or stapler, and, for every child, scissors, pen, crayons or markers, 1 photocopy of the "Rights and Responsibilities" handout (p. 113) preferably copied on card stock; optional, flat plastic jewelry, glue and/or glitter crayons

Say: **Being a prince or princess can be great, but it can be tough, too. King David had the love and respect of thousands of people, but he also had to go out and fight wars. When you wear a crown, you have rights *and* responsibilities. You are princes and princesses, children of the King! God chose you out of all the people on earth to be his treasures. But God asks you to act like kingdom kids. He said, "If you obey me fully, you will be my kingdom leaders."** (See Exodus 19:5-6.)

Have the kids use pen to write, "God's treasured people choose to obey," on the flip side of the crown. They can color and decorate the crown with plastic jewelry. Staple each child's crown to fit his or her head. Have kids parade around the room wearing their crowns, while you read to them from Deuteronomy 10:12-15 from *The Living Bible*.

(20 minutes)
Choices of the Chosen

In this activity, children will review the commandments by acting them out.

Items to Pack: 10 index cards, pen

Write each of the Ten Commandments on a different index card, letting the kids say them as your write them. Have the kids form groups of three or four, making sure that the younger kids are on teams with older kids. Give each group commandment cards. Depending on how many groups you have, you may need to give some groups more than two cards. Each team is to tell and act out a short story about a child who was tempted to break the commandment it has. The other kids are to guess which commandment the skit or story is about. For example, a team can make up a story about a girl who was so busy with ballet lessons that she forgot about God. After each correct guess, reiterate the point, saying, ⬤ "God's treasured people choose to obey him."

(15 minutes)
Top Ten Team

In this activity, the children will design T-shirts for God's elect.

Items to Pack: T-shirt with a logo from a recognized sports team (or a baseball hat or some other item from a recognized team), and, for each child, blank paper, pen, crayons

Hold up the T-shirt and ask:

• **If I wear this shirt, what does this say about me?**

• **How is being God's treasured people like being on a team?**

Say: **God said that we are ⬤ his treasured people, and we show that we are his treasured people when we choose to obey. We can cheer each other on to obey God's laws.**

Hand children blank sheets of paper, and show them how to draw the simple outline of a T-shirt. Ask them to design a T-shirt for the class that shows they all agree to keep God's laws. Some ideas for names are "Kingdom Kids," "Covenant Club," "Commandment Keepers," and "Top Ten Team." Share their design ideas with the group.

You can take one of the designs to a T-shirt store and ask them to print it on T-shirts that the kids can wear on the last day of class, or you can buy transfer paper at a craft store to put the design on T-shirts yourself. Or use fabric marker to write the selected name on individual T-shirts, and let the kids make handprints with both hands dipped in fabric paint.

TOUR GUIDE TIP

When reviewing these commandments, show the children that the first four commandments deal with our relationship to God. They can be summarized by Jesus' answer to the question, "What is the most important commandment?" His answer was, "Love the Lord your God with all your heart and with all your soul and with all your mind and with all your strength." The second part of Jesus' answer was "Love your neighbor as yourself." This addresses the rest of the commandments, which deal with our relationships to others.

Items to Pack: the poster from the "God's Dream Come True" activity

Items to Pack: the crowns from the "Rights and Responsibilities of the Crown" activity, poster board, marker

TRAVEL-ALONG COMMANDMENT SONG

(10 minutes)

Teach kids this last stanza. Break the kids up into teams of ten, if possible. Have each team memorize the song and motions.

Assign each team one of the stanzas, and tell them to stand up to do the motions when it's their turn. See pages 6-8 to review the full song.

To show God your love, come on, try to obey. *(Hold hands out.)*

But when you mess up, God shows the way. *(Cover face with hands, then move hands away.)*

The commandments point us to the cross. *(Point up.)*

Jesus died for you. Now make him your boss. *(Make a cross.)*

ONE WAY (10 minutes)

The Big Problem With a Little Word

In this activity, the children will realize that they are disqualified but not hopeless.

Have all the kids stand in front of the poster. Ask them to go through God's commandments one at a time. After each commandment, ask them if they have always obeyed it.

Say: **God said that you would be his treasured people. If you haven't obeyed, take your name off the poster, and lay it on the ground.**

After you've gone through all the commandments and all names have been taken off, ask:

• **What happens when you are separated from God?**

Say: **It looks hopeless. God gives us laws, and even though we try, we still break them. But listen to this. "But now God has shown us a different way to heaven—not by 'being good enough' and trying to keep his laws, but by a new way (though not new, really, for the Scriptures told about it long ago). Now God says he will accept and acquit us—declare us 'not guilty'—if we trust Jesus Christ to take away our sins...no matter who we are or what we have been like"** (Romans 3:21-22 *TLB*).

Now turn your name over, and write on the back: "I am God's treasure." Take your paper home with you as a reminder to trust Jesus to take away your sins.

HOME AGAIN PRAYER

(10 minutes)

Put one chair for each child in a circle facing in. Leave a space in the circle for children to go in and out. Put a crown on each chair. Tell the children that the circle represents God's castle. Use the poster board as a drawbridge.

Say: **Jesus Christ laid down his life** (lay down the poster board, and draw a cross on it) **to bring you to God.**

Read 1 Peter 3:18. Have the kids walk over the drawbridge, enter God's kingdom, and wear their crowns as you say the following prayer:

Dear King Jesus, thank you so much for laying down your life to bring me to God. Thank you for choosing me to be your special treasure. I choose to obey you. When I am tempted to break your loving laws, please help me to remember that I am a child of God. Amen.

Rights and Responsibilities

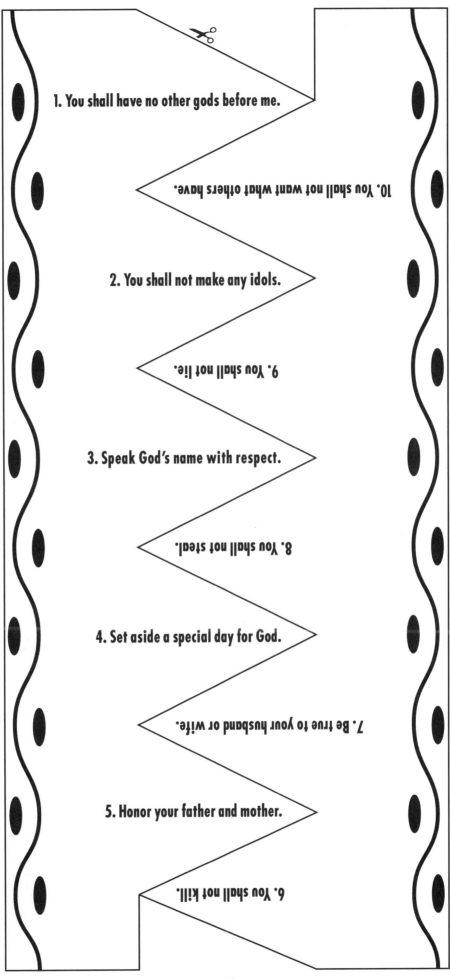

1. You shall have no other gods before me.

10. You shall not want what others have.

2. You shall not make any idols.

9. You shall not lie.

3. Speak God's name with respect.

8. You shall not steal.

4. Set aside a special day for God.

7. Be true to your husband or wife.

5. Honor your father and mother.

6. You shall not kill.

The Law Leads Us to the Cross

Pathway Point: 🌑 Our sin is real, but our sin is gone!

In-Focus Verse: "The more we know of God's laws, the clearer it becomes that we aren't obeying them; his laws serve only to make us see that we are sinners" (Romans 3: 20b, *TLB*).

Travel Itinerary

Why did nature convulse on Mount Sinai? When God handed Moses those two cold stone slabs, innocence was slain. From that moment until the crucifixion, Israel stood hushed and guilty before Almighty God. (See Romans 3:19.) This is the work and purpose of the Law. But the story doesn't end with our failures. James Schaap expressed this simple but profound truth, "The blessing of the Gospel is not simply our happiness but eternal joy that...comes from two humbling realizations—that our sin is real, and that it is gone."

Gone! Vanished! Poof! "God sent Christ Jesus to take the punishment for our sins and to end all God's anger against us" (Romans 3:25a, *TLB*). Doesn't that make you want to shout? The entire Bible can be summarized into "Our sin is real"—the Old Testament—and "Our sin is gone!"—the New Testament. Share this incredible joy with the children.

DEPARTURE PRAYER (5 minutes)

Today's lesson is the most important one. Spend some time on your knees asking God's Holy Spirit to illuminate the children's minds. You may want to ask several parents to pray with you before class. All the creative lessons in the world can't substitute for the Spirit's power in bringing a child to Christ. See 1 Corinthians 2:1-5.

Dear Lord God, please help me to show the children through the Ten Commandments that their sin is real. Help them to see where they've fallen short of your desires. Help them to see their sin and their need for the Savior, Jesus! Thank you for sending your Son to break the chains of our disobedience. Dear Jesus, thank you for dying in our place and rising again. Because of the Ten Commandments, we know our sin is real. Because of you, Jesus, our sin is *gone!* Thank you. Amen.

1st STOP DISCOVERY (15 minutes) Sin In, Sin Gone!

In this activity, children will pour water into a cup and watch it disappear, like our sin.

Preparation: Try this at home first.

Even little kids can work this trick of "disappearing" water. Before class, take the diaper, and tear off the outer layer. Stuff the diaper lining into the cup, filling the cup about half full. Try to not let the kids see over the top of your cup.

Say: **Let's say that this cup is me, and this water is my sin. I have broken God's loving laws.** Go through each commandment, letting the kids help you name them. After each commandment, pour a little water into the cup, saying, for example: **I have sinned. I have not always given God first place in my life. Sometimes I take more time with** [name a specific person or thing] **than with God.**

After going through all the commandments say: **I am full of sin, just as this cup is full of water, like a prisoner condemned to die. But then Jesus came and died on the cross for me.** Draw a cross on the cup. **He took my sins away! My sin is real.** Turn the cup over, squeezing it slightly. **My sin is gone!**

Ask:

• **How did the water disappear?**

• **How does Jesus take away our sins?**

• **Is your sin real? Is your sin gone? How do you know?**

Use these Scripture verses to review a few basics of salvation: Romans 8:16; 1 John 1:9; and 1 John 5:11-12. Let each child perform the same "trick," saying, "My sin is real." Then have them turn their cups over and say, "My sin is gone!"

Items to Pack: for each child, foam cup, pen, water; for every 3 or 4 kids, disposable diaper

STORY EXCURSION (20 minutes)
Dallas Understands

Preparation: Tape each of the commandments to a different chair, and set the chairs around the room in the order of the commandments. Place the permanent marker and the bucket of water at the end. To give you the opportunity to talk to kids about their relationship with Jesus, ask one or two other adults to continue with the activities listed under "Adventure in Living God's Laws." Take the kids out of the room individually to talk after the story.

Items to Pack: each of the Ten Commandments written on paper, red washable marker, red permanent marker, bucket of sudsy water, towel

Ask the kids to follow you from one chair to the next. If they've disobeyed the commandment on that chair, mark one of their fingers with a dot of red washable marker. Start with the left thumb, and proceed until you mark the tenth commandment on the right thumb. Mark your own fingers as the story unfolds.

Say: **There was a boy named Dallas. He was a lot like most people. When I asked Dallas, "If you died tonight, would you go to heaven?" Dallas answered, "Yes, I guess so." When I asked him why God would let him into heaven, Dallas said, "I'm pretty good. I mean, I've never killed anybody, and I don't steal."**

Let's see if Dallas' good is good enough for God's standards. Go to the first chair, and have the kids repeat the commandment found there. **Dallas realized that he didn't always worship God alone. "Oh, yeah," Dallas said. "Once I prayed to an angel to help me make a free throw." Have you ever prayed to or worshipped anyone but God?** After the children admit that they have, mark on their left thumbs.

Go to the next chair, and have the kids repeat the commandment found there. **Dallas didn't think he had made any idols. But he realized that sometimes he loved his** video games even more than God. How about you? Have you always put God first in your life? Mark kids' left index fingers.

Go to the next chair, and have the children repeat the commandment found there. Dallas had an older brother named Dan. Dan only thought Dallas was cool when he used bad language. It had become a bad habit with Dallas. Have you ever spoken God's name in an ugly way? Have you ever said a swear word? Mark kids' fingers.

Go to the next chair, and have the children repeat the commandment found there. On Sundays, Dallas went to church—sometimes. Most of the time, he went fishing. Sometimes a whole month would slip by without his setting aside a special day for God. Have you always remembered and worshipped God? Mark kids' fingers.

Go to the next chair, and have the children repeat the commandment found there. Dallas didn't even have to think hard about this commandment. He knew that he didn't always obey his parents. Sometimes he was sassy to his mom. Have you always respected and obeyed your parents? Mark kids' fingers.

Go to the next chair, and have the children repeat the commandment found there. "Phew," Dallas thought. "I've never killed anyone." Then he remembered shouting, "Kill him!" when he played his video game. "Oops, I guess in a way, I've even broken that commandment." Ask the kids if they have ever been a part of saying yes to violence or no to life. Mark their fingers.

Go to the next chair, and have the children repeat the commandment found there. Dallas was starting to wish he had never been asked all these questions. It was as if a flashlight were shining into his secret soul. Dallas was happy to learn that God's seventh commandment was, "Be true to your husband or wife." He decided he'd just never get married when he grew up. But when I explained that this commandment was about keeping all your promises, he held out his hand to get finger number seven marked. Have you kept all your promises? Mark kids' fingers.

Go to the next chair, and have the children read the commandment found there. Dallas knew the eighth commandment was "You shall not steal." "Yes, OK, once I stole my sister's gum. But she...never mind, just mark my finger," Dallas said. Ask the kids if they've been getters instead of givers, and mark their fingers.

Go to the next chair, and have the children read the commandment found there. Dallas was beginning to wish he could run away and jump into a bathtub. He had broken God's ninth commandment, "You shall not lie," lots of times, even though he knew that it's always best to tell the truth. His hands were getting very dirty. Have you always told the truth? Mark kids' fingers.

Go to the last chair, and have the children read the commandment found there. When we got to the last commandment, "You shall not want what others have," Dallas couldn't stop thinking about Mark Jacob's four-wheeler. "Oh, boy, I'm breaking this commandment even while I'm learning about it!" He hung his head and mumbled, "I guess I'm just hopeless." Then he stood there, without saying another word. Ask the kids if they've ever wanted what others have. Mark their fingers.

Ask:

• How does Dallas feel about himself?

• How do you feel about yourself?

Read this paraphrase of Romans 3:10-20: **There is not one person who is right with God. We all have turned away. We all have sinned. In fact, all the world stands hushed, dirty, and guilty before Almighty God. The more we know of God's laws, the clearer it becomes that we aren't obeying them. His laws serve to make us see that we are sinners. Our sin is real.**

We would be without hope if it weren't for two other red marks on the hands of someone who never broke even one of God's commandments. Jesus Christ came to earth to die for your sins and mine. Put a mark in the center of each of your hands with the red permanent marker. **Jesus let soldiers nail him to the cross. Since he was perfect, without any sin, God said that his death would pay for our sins. Our sin is real, but because of Jesus, our sin is** (wash your hands in the bucket) *gone!*

Have the children look at their hands and say, "Our sin is real." Have them wash their hands and say, "Our sin is gone!" Only the two permanent ink marks will remain.

Use the following activity time to talk individually with the kids. Ask them the two questions about heaven from the beginning of the story to see if they understand the concepts of sin and forgiveness.

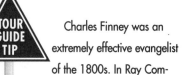

Charles Finney was an extremely effective evangelist of the 1800s. In Ray Comfort's *Hell's Best Kept Secret,* Finney is quoted as saying "Bring up the individual's particular sins. Talking in general terms against sin will produce no results."

Be sure to let the kids help you name specific violations of each commandment. By doing this, one child will relate with another and see his or her sin for what it is.

ADVENTURE IN LIVING GOD'S LAWS

(10 minutes)
Disappearing Sin

This simple paperwork illustrates our vanquished sin problem.

Have the kids form pairs to discuss the following questions:
• **Why did God give us the Ten Commandments?**
• **What happens to the people who can't keep them?**
• **How does God help us since we can't keep them all?**

Say: **God gave us the Ten Commandments to show us that our sin is real.** (See Romans 3:19-20 and Matthew 5:17.) **Since we can't keep all his laws, God sent his Son, Jesus, to do for us what we can't do. God knows that our sin is real. But because of Jesus, our sin is gone!**

Have the kids fold the page vertically, print side facing out. Have them cut out the tablets, and use the marker to write in large letters right across the commandments, "Our sin is real." Then have them draw a cross. Under the cross, have them write, "Our sin is..." Then have them fold the page so the commandments are inside. On the blank side of the paper, have them write "GONE!" in disappearing glue. Let the younger kids just write "GONE!"

Items to Pack: a few glue sticks that go on purple and dry clear, and, for each child, 1 light photocopy of the stone tablets (p. 9), scissors, markers

(15 minutes)
The Law as a White Glove

In this activity, children will try to clean up their own acts.

Have the kids clean a defined area, asking them to straighten, sweep, and dust while you are out of the room for a few minutes. When they have finished, admire their work,

Items to Pack: flashlight, white cleaning rags or paper towels, broom

saying, "It looks very clean. Good job!" Then bring out the flashlight and start inspecting more closely. Give it the "white glove" treatment with a damp white cloth, especially in the corners. Show the kids the dust you collected.

Ask:

• **Why didn't you notice this dust?**

• **How are this flashlight and white rag like God's commandments?**

• **What does our sin look like under God's holy light?**

Say: **In the story, Dallas thought he was pretty good. But when he started looking at all of God's commandments, his good actions were actually pretty dirty. This is why God gave us his commandments, to make us see that our sin is real. But because of Jesus, our sin is** (throw the rag away) *gone!* **When Jesus forgives us, we look like a clean, unused, white cloth!**

(10 minutes)
Sugar, Sugar

In this activity, children will watch sugar cubes disappear, just as our sins disappear.

Items to Pack: for each child, a sugar cube, plus a sugar cube for yourself

Before children arrive, warm a large pot of water. It needs to be hot—but not scalding. And you'll need a way to comfortably and safely stir the water.

Gather children around the pot and give each child a sugar cube. Say: **Our sin is real. We know that from these many weeks of studying God's commandments. But when Jesus forgives us, our sin is gone. He throws our sin away.** Read this paraphrase of Psalm 103:11-12: **For as high as the heavens are above the earth, so great is God's love for us. As far as the east is from the west, that's how far God throws away our sin.** Toss a sugar cube into the water. It'll quickly dissolve as you stir. Say: **My sin is real. But because of God's love** (continue stirring) **my sin is gone—melted—history!**

Invite children to one at a time drop their sugar cubes into the water as you stir. As they do so, ask them to silently identify one sin for which they need forgiveness, and to ask God to forgive them.

Items to Pack: several glue sticks, and, for each child, 1 photocopy of the sunglasses (p. 120), scissors, pen

SOUVENIRS → (20 minutes)
Eyes to See

In this activity, the children will make lift-the-flap glasses for their new eyes that see the truth.

Preparation: Cut out the inner parts of the sunglasses for each child before class. This will save valuable class time and prevent rips. You may want to cut out the earpieces for the younger kids. Make a pair of glasses for yourself.

Have the kids cut out the glasses and the earpieces. Have them fold the earpieces on the dotted lines and glue the folded flaps to the front of the glasses. On the front left flap of the glasses, have the kids write, "Our sin"; on the right flap, "is real." Then have them lift the flaps and write on the inside of the left flap, "Our sin"; on the inside of the right flap, "is gone."

Ask:

- How is not knowing God's laws like having blinders on?
- How can we lift the blinders to see the truth?
- When was the truth of God's laws made real to you?

To help answer these questions, put on your glasses, and have a child read Romans 3:20b in *The Living Bible*: "The more we know of God's laws, the clearer it becomes that we aren't obeying them; his laws serve only to make us see that we are sinners." When we believe in Jesus and say we're sorry for breaking God's laws, our very real sin becomes very gone sin. It's like the veil that we talked about last week. Let the kids repeat what they've written on the glasses while wearing them and lifting the flaps up.

TRAVEL-ALONG COMMANDMENT SONG

(10 minutes)

All-Gone Song

Children will sing this rap song that rejoices over our forgiveness.

Preparation: Practice this song until you memorize it.

Celebrate a clean slate! Get a good rhythm going for this rap song, and rock from one foot to the other. For the last two lines, take a child by the hand to join you. That child will take another hand, and so on, until everyone is partying together.

Our sin is real. *(Clap. Put hands in front of face, palms in.)*

Our sin is gone. *(Clap. Turn hands out.)*

So come on up. *(Clap to the left.)*

Let's sing this song. *(Clap to the right.)*

Hey, party, party, party, party! *(Take a child's hand to join you. Then clap above your head.)*

Hey, party, party, party, party! *(Clap above and then wiggle fingers moving hands down.)*

Repeat until all the kids have joined in.

SCENIC ROUTE →

Teach this song to some teens in your church, and ask them to help you sing it with the kids. This will encourage some reluctant fourth- and fifth-grade boys who really do want to join the party but think they're too cool. Bring some confetti, and throw it on each child who joins the party line. Or you can assign the confetti-throwing job to the just-too-shy-to-dance kid.

HOME AGAIN PRAYER

(5 minutes)

In this prayer, the children will see sin disappears as they pray for forgiveness.

Have the kids gather in a circle. Ask them each to put a smudge of charcoal on their faces. Say: **Sometimes we can't see our own sin, just as we can't see the smudges on our faces, but everyone else can. And of course, God sees all our sin.** During this prayer, while everyone's eyes are closed, quietly wipe away the smudge on your own face when you say the words, "Our sin is gone."

Dear Lord, our God, what can we say to a God as great as you? You are holy, perfect, and wonderful. We are full of sin. We break your commandments. Forgive us. You don't change the commandments to make it easier for us, and you don't leave us hopeless. You paid the price for our disobedience by sending your Son, Jesus, to take away our sins. Yes, Lord, our sin is real. Thank you, Jesus, that our sin is gone! We'll love you forever. Thank you for your loving laws that keep us safe and show us how much we need you. Amen.

Items to Pack: for each child, wet wipe, piece of charcoal

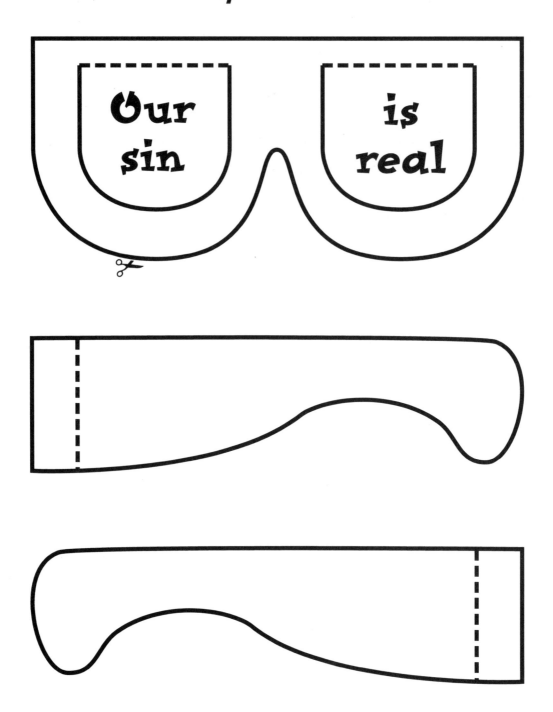

Our sin

is real